HALF EMPTY

An Interpretive Guide to Ecclesiastes

BY
A. WENDELL BOWES

f⁃

THE FOUNDRY
PUBLISHING®

The Foundry Publishing®
PO Box 419527
Kansas City, MO 64141
thefoundrypublishing.com

ISBN 978-0-8341-4324-1

Printed in the
United States of America

Cover design: Caines Design
Interior design: Sharon Page

Library of Congress Cataloging-in-Publication Data
A complete catalog record for this book is available from the Library of Congress.

10 9 8 7 6 5 4 3 2 1

To
Simon and Johonah,
may you always live lives of goodness and wisdom
guided by the Sages' advice
in Proverbs and Ecclesiastes.

CONTENTS

AUTHOR'S PREFACE

I started this book and its companion volume on Proverbs after writing *The Wisdom Literature* (Bowes 2024). In the process of my research for that book, I discovered that the resources for preaching from Proverbs and Ecclesiastes were extremely limited. Some commentators even discouraged trying to produce such resources. I accepted that as a challenge and began writing.

In hindsight, I probably bit off more than I could chew. Writing on Proverbs was a delight. So many topics in this book beg for consideration. It is a very practical guidebook for successful living. But Ecclesiastes was more difficult. I really struggled to find material that would be appropriate for the pulpit. The sermon resources I developed are worthy of consideration, but the effort was challenging. I hope preachers and teachers find my sermon-starter proposals helpful and will make the effort to use these biblical books in their ministry.

While driving around my community, I recently found myself following a car with a decal on its rear window: "Life Is Good." I wanted to stop the driver and learn the reasons for her optimism. But not wanting to be mistaken for a stalker, I instead began to ponder in my own mind whether I could make the same evaluation about my own life. I can honestly say that life overall has been good to me. Yes, there have been times of great distress and frustration. There have been times of financial concern. There have been times of sorrow and grief. I imagine there will be more such times in the years ahead. But overall, life is good. Physically, I am still kicking, but at a much slower pace. Intellectually, my mind still functions fairly well.

The titles of these two volumes (*Half Full* and *Half Empty*) attempt to highlight the major differences in people's outlooks on life. These differences are nowhere more evident than in the books of Proverbs and Ecclesiastes. The authors of both books were seeking the same goal—to find the meaning of life and to enable them to live successfully. They used the same resources in their research—observations of nature and human behavior, insights passed down from previous generations of sages, and instructions from God. Interestingly, these authors came to very different conclusions. In doing so, they illustrate the differences in how people look at life today.

The authors and collectors who created *Proverbs* were able to look on the bright side of life, emphasizing the good things they saw around them and the blessings God provides those who serve him. They were optimistic because they believed life would always go well for those who fear God (Prov. 11:27). They produced and preserved sayings that were happy and confident about life lived in God's will.

In contrast, the author and editor of *Ecclesiastes* were troubled by life's problems and senselessness. They had seen too many instances of bad things happening to good people. They were troubled by God's silence when people most needed him to make sense of their experiences. They felt they were wandering in a dark wilderness, because they could not find the key to life's meaning. Consequently, they skeptically questioned whether any human being could ever understand the overall purpose of life. To them, life was not good; life was just vanity.

Such differences in perspective are still evident today. Many people have an optimistic mindset. Others, including believers, are constantly pessimistic. Such differences may be due to personality traits and upbringing. At other times, they are caused by differences in life's experiences. Imagine how inexplicable tragedies can turn people's lives topsy-turvy—dealing with the senseless death of a child in a school mass shooting, having to place a spouse in a memory-care facility, losing one's life savings to an identity thief. Such people would probably claim that life had not been good to them. They might feel they were living under a shadow that never went away.

Whatever the cause, we need to evaluate where we stand on the scale of optimism versus pessimism. We may need to make some adjustments or course corrections. We all want to live a good life. We all want to be successful in our families, our jobs, and our relationships.

We all want to enjoy good health and good finances. But sometimes our basic approach to life is overly optimistic (Proverbs) or overly pessimistic (Ecclesiastes). We fail to see life realistically, if we do not see it as God sees it.

Qohelet, the author of Ecclesiastes, had it about right when he encouraged his students to follow the golden mean—the middle pathway between the extremes (Eccles. 7:15-18). Somewhere in the middle is where he thought people should live. Modern culture would profit from that message.

The people in ancient times who produced the biblical canon have sometimes been criticized for including a book like Ecclesiastes. Its critics say it is simply too skeptical for Christians to read. They want people always to think positive thoughts, like those in Proverbs. But maybe the ancients were wiser than we give them credit for being. They certainly knew that Proverbs would be a popular book because it promises rewards to everyone who follows its advice. They also knew that life has its dark moments, when the sun disappears for days, weeks, months, even years at a time. Sometimes confusion and despair bring us to a crisis of faith. Saints have called such times the "dark night of the soul" (following John of the Cross).

Ecclesiastes offers a much-needed corrective to unrealistic optimism. It speaks to these darker moments and honestly asks questions that need to be considered. Therefore, wisely, the ancients included it in the canon alongside Proverbs. Hopefully, preachers and teachers today will follow their lead and include both these books in their preaching schedule. We all need to hear the profound messages that Proverbs and Ecclesiastes have provided people over the centuries.

—Wendell Bowes

COMPILER'S PREFACE

My dad—A. Wendell Bowes—had a passion for church congregations to read, understand, and learn from the entire Bible. This included all the books in the Old Testament (OT). It was important to him that congregations be biblically literate so that they could personally know the Lord and grow deeply in their faith.

For this to happen, preachers would need to preach from the entire Bible regularly. They needed to help congregations understand the books of the Bible and how these apply to their lives today. Again, this included the Old Testament. Because for many people the OT is more challenging to understand than the New Testament (NT), it often gets neglected in preaching schedules. Therefore, Dad sometimes referred to his desire as a "one-man campaign."

This did not stop him from making his contribution to this cause. As you will read in appendix A at the conclusion of the book, he pastored churches, taught as a university professor to prepare students for pastoral ministry, and studied, researched, and wrote on various biblical subjects. Upon "retiring," his third career was writing books for pastors, preachers, and teachers about the OT wisdom literature. This book is his fifth.

Ecclesiastes 9:12 reads, "No one knows when their hour will come." This proved true for the author of this book. A couple weeks after asking me to read the draft on Proverbs, the companion volume to this book, he died very unexpectedly without any illness. The Lord ordained that this was *his* "time to die" (3:2).

Sharing his wish and desire to see his final manuscript published, I gathered his files and notes to compile and edit it. I, too, desire–and need–to understand the books of the Bible through good preaching and teaching for my own walk with God. With my mom's (mentioned later in the book as Ginger) shorthand and proofreading skills, Dad's now two-volume work is complete.[1]

In the process, an unsolved mystery emerged. In the introduction to Ecclesiastes Dad wrote, "My book contains seven sermon starters," and indeed it does. However, the files to seven other divisions of Ecclesiastes remained empty. Missing comments on Ecclesiastes 5–8 and 10–11:6 and a partially written epilogue (12:9-14) have left us wondering. What did he intend to write in these chapters? More sermon starters? More explanations? We will never know.

For seventeen years, he studied and wrote his own OT Sunday school lessons for an adult class taught weekly at his local church. He also had taught college classes on all the books of the OT. His notes on Ecclesiastes from these lessons and classes were available and, therefore, have been included in chapter 9, "Additional Sermon Ideas from Ecclesiastes." These will provide a starting point for preaching and teaching from these divisions. His intent was for people to use his work for learning and developing their own sermons. These are his notes for you to do so.

Ironically, Dad had completed the chapter titled "Death Awaits Us All" shortly before his death. As our family grieves his loss, this volume has been a great comfort to me as we received his last words of wisdom.

I couldn't help but notice the unforeseen and unusual similarity of Qohelet and the Ecclesiastes editor to Dad, George Lyons, and me. Both original authors had assistance to bring their wisdom to people. Dad's longtime colleague and friend George Lyons edited the final draft of the book. He was ably assisted by two of Dad's former students, both now with doctoral degrees in Old Testament studies, Marty Michelson and Ben Boeckel, who checked all the transliterations of words in Hebrew and other Semitic languages. Thanks to all those who assisted in bringing this unfinished project to completion. This includes the folks at the Foundry, who have allowed Dad's final book to "see the light of day."

—Heidi Bowes

---

1. The publisher divided the original manuscript into two volumes—one on Proverbs and the other on Ecclesiastes.

ABBREVIATIONS

General

→	see another part of the book at
AD	anno Domini (precedes date)
ANE	ancient Near East(ern)
BC	before Christ (follows date)
c.	century
ca.	*circa*, around
cf.	compare
ch(s).	chapter(s)
ed(s).	editor(s); edition
e.g.	*exempli gratia*, for example
esp.	especially
etc.	*et cetera*, and the rest
HB	Hebrew Bible
ibid.	*ibidem*, in the same place
i.e.	*id est*, in other words, that is
l(l).	line(s)
lit.	literally
no(s).	number(s)
NT	New Testament
OT	Old Testament
repr.	reprint, reprinted
trans.	translated by
v(v).	verse(s)
vol(s).	volume(s)

Modern English Bible Translations

AT	author's translation
GNT	Good News Translation (Today's English Version)
KJV	King James Version
MSG	The Message
NASB	New American Standard Bible
NIV	New International Version (2011 ed.)
NIV[1984]	New International Version (1984 ed.)
NJPS	Tanakh: The Holy Scriptures: The New Jewish Publication Society Translation

NRSV	New Revised Standard Version
Phillips	*The New Testament in Modern English* (J. B. Phillips)
REB	Revised English Bible
TLB	The Living Bible

Modern Reference Works

ABD	*Anchor Bible Dictionary* (see Freedman)
AEL	*Ancient Egyptian Literature: A Book of Readings* (see Lichtheim)
ANET	*Ancient Near Eastern Texts Relating to the Old Testament* (see Pritchard)

INTRODUCTION

The book of Ecclesiastes is seldom used in Christian ministry, even less than Proverbs. Few Christians are familiar with its message. Most preachers avoid it because they are uncomfortable with its skeptical, cynical tone. What can we do with this strange book? Did the author really believe that all of life is meaningless (Eccles. 1:2), or was he trying to warn people against this type of thinking? One valid reason for preachers' hesitation about using Ecclesiastes in the pulpit or teachers' hesitation in the classroom is the wide range of interpretations by commentators. Almost every scholar has a different viewpoint.

> Is the author incoherent, insightful or confused? Is he a stark realist or merely faithless? Is he orthodox or heterodox? Is he an optimist or a pessimist? Is the final message of the book "Be like Qohelet [the author of Ecclesiastes], the wise man" or "Qohelet is wrong, so do not fall into his trap"? (Enns 2008, 121)

There are scholars who support each of the above options, leading Seow to make this comment: "There is perhaps no book in the Bible that is the subject of more controversies than Ecclesiastes" (1997, ix). In this book, I try to avoid the major controversies and focus on some passages and themes that offer good preaching value.

Preliminary Considerations

Allow me to repeat some general principles I suggested in my earlier book on preaching and teaching from the book of Job (Bowes 2021, 14-18). I have also added several details here that apply especially to Ecclesiastes.

1. Invest in Some Good Commentaries

A good library of resources is essential for constructing effective sermons and lessons. Ideally, one should have five or six commentaries on hand for each biblical book. These should include at least one that is theological in nature and one that focuses on accurately translating and interpreting the Hebrew text. The commentaries on Ecclesiastes that I turn to most frequently are Bennett, Brown, Fox, Longman, Murphy, Seow, and Towner. See the list of references at the end of the book for further suggestions.

2. Make Use of Several Different Bible Versions That Employ Different Theories of Translation

Bible translations seem to be a problem for some pastors, so here are some comments to help resolve the confusion. There are many good versions of the Bible on the market today. Laypeople are often perplexed about which to buy for themselves or as a gift for a family member. Too often, decisions are based on the color or quality of the cover. When asked, I usually encourage people to tell me what is important to them in choosing a Bible. The following are some questions that need to be answered first.

a. What Are You Going to Use the Bible For?

Is this a Bible for devotional reading? For writing sermons and college term papers? For a Bible study group? For memorization? Or is this a gift for your elementary child or teenager? There are versions appropriate for every use.

b. How Literal a Translation Do You Want?

Are you looking for a literal translation that is as close to the original Hebrew and Greek texts as possible? A contemporary translation that uses modern language and grammar? A completely free version that attempts to convey ideas clearly rather than accurately rendering individual words? Some paraphrases of the Bible have not consulted the original Hebrew and Greek.

c. With What English Format Are You Comfortable?

There was almost no formatting in the original biblical texts. Modern versions attempt to make translations more user friendly in appearance. Do you want distinctions made between poetry and prose sections? Do you want inserted editorial headings and paragraph divisions? Capitalized pronouns referring to God? The words of Jesus in red?

d. *How Do You Want to Read Weights, Measures, Monetary Units, and Calendar Designations?*

Are you happy with the original Hebrew words such as "shekels," "talents," "cubits," "homers," and months like "Nisan"? Or would you prefer conversions into English equivalents such as "dollars," "pounds," "kilograms," "inches," "meters," "quarts," and months like "April"? Regarding modern monetary units, readers must be aware that these change over time because of inflation.

e. *How Do You Prefer the Version to Treat Words Referring to Sexual Parts of the Body and Bathroom Activities?*

Would you rather that your Bible contain a euphemism or a word that is accurate but graphic? Compare Genesis 31:35 in the NRSV and NIV for an example of each.

f. *How Do You Want the Version to Treat Gendered Language?*

Many translations today use plural pronouns (such as "they," "them," "themselves") in texts that refer to all people, not just males. But the plural changes the reference to the number of people mentioned. For example, compare the more literal rendering of Mark 4:25 in the NASB with the gender-neutral rendering in the NRSV.

g. *Does It Matter If the Version Was Translated by a Committee or an Individual?*

Most versions were translated by a select committee of biblical scholars, but a few (such as The Message, *The New Testament in Modern English* [Phillips], and The Living Bible) were crafted by one person. Theological biases are more apt to appear in a single-person translation.

h. *Do You Want Only the Printed Biblical Text, or Do You Want the Additional Resources Provided by Study Bibles?*

Study Bibles include maps, notes at the foot of each page, and explanations at the beginning of each book. They also usually include cross-references to quotations and possible allusions in other biblical passages.

As you think about the Bible versions that you are going to use in sermon or lesson preparation, be aware that no one translation perfectly satisfies all your wishes. Each has strengths and weaknesses. Therefore, choose several translations that offer a wide variety of renderings of each text.

The versions I turn to most frequently are the NRSV (fairly literal), GNT (free), NIV (dynamically equivalent), and the NJPS (Jewish). The translators of each version used a different set of principles to guide their translations. That is refreshing and helpful.

3. Give Yourself Adequate Time for Preparation

The book of Ecclesiastes is one of the most difficult books to preach from in the entire Bible. Its pessimistic attitude has frustrated many preachers. Nevertheless, don't let that turn you away from a book that has rich spiritual resources for modern times. It just means that you will need to spend a significant amount of time in preparation. Preachers and teachers will need to do a lot of reading in commentaries and spend a lot of time thinking and meditating about what this book is saying.

4. Take Advantage of the Timeless Nature of the Wisdom Books

All the wisdom books are timeless in nature. Job forces us to think about unjust suffering. Ecclesiastes challenges us with trying to find meaning in a world that often is unfair, contradictory, and unexplainable. Proverbs gives us insights into how to live well. These are basic human issues that transcend time, geography, race, and gender. They are just as relevant today as when they were first written. This timelessness provides preachers and teachers with a multitude of fascinating topics.

5. Decide on the Interpretive Method You Are Going to Use

Probably the most important task that preachers and teachers need to consider before beginning a sermon or lesson is to decide on the appropriate method of interpretation. Are you going to treat Ecclesiastes negatively (1) as an illustration of how *not* to think and live, (2) as the reflections of a secular rather than spiritual mind, or (3) as irrelevant to the main message of the OT? Many have followed each approach.

Some early Christian writers saw the author's emphasis on vanity as a true description of the secular world. This led them literally to reject human society and support the movement toward asceticism, following Paul's admonition in Colossians 3:1-2. Others were so turned off by the skeptical attitude of the author that they resorted to an allegorical approach using the references to eating and drinking (such as Eccles. 2:24-26) as support for the Eucharist. Wesley thought that Solomon wrote it toward the end of his life to warn people against living a meaningless life as he had done (1765, 3:1893). More recently, some have treated Ecclesiastes, not as contributing to the message of the OT, but as a foil to be criticized and improved upon by the NT. They have interpreted it "as the dark background against which the light of the gospel shines forth" (Towner 1997, 267). Such negative methods leave readers with a bad attitude toward the book. They may even wonder whether it belongs in the Bible.

Other interpreters are much more positive in their evaluation of the book. They are open to treating the book as a legitimate part of the canon that has much to offer contemporary human beings. For example, in the time of the Reformation, scholars such as Luther believed that the book encouraged the enjoyment of life. Gordis echoes this thought: "Thus the basic theme of the book is its insistence upon the enjoyment of life, of all the good things in the world" (1968, 124).

A common approach today is to view the book as a serious and realistic questioning of the prevailing view of the sages that life will always go well for us if we fear God and do his will. This idea, as encouraged in Proverbs, was too simplistic in the view of the author of Ecclesiastes. For him, life does not always go well for human beings, and we usually do not know why.

Another book in the wisdom literature also struggled to make sense of life. Job was the most saintly person of his generation (Job 1:1, 8). Yet he still suffered horrendous tragedies and loss that caused him to question everything about his life, including God's relationship with him. The author of Ecclesiastes raises questions that are similar to Job's. However, his questions apply more to the human condition in general than they do to his own personal losses.

Among modern biblical scholars, Childs has led the way in trying to rehabilitate the reputation of Ecclesiastes. He says that the book is not just the "individual quirks" of a confused author who stands alone and outside the mainstream of Israelite theology. Rather, it functions as a "critical corrective" to other parts of the wisdom literature, such as the happy, little sayings in Proverbs. It provides a valid, alternative view, "much as the book of James serves in the New Testament as an essential corrective to misunderstanding the Pauline letters" (1979, 588).

Brown, too, attempts to interpret the book as a legitimate part of the canon. He proposes integrating the book into Christian theology by treating it as an example of "faith seeking understanding."

> If anything, Qohelet emphasizes the "seeking" dimension that is essential to faithful inquiry. As a seeker, Qohelet sees himself on a journey toward understanding the totality of existence under God, of making sense of the world through the eyes of faith. Such an endeavor strikes at the heart and process of theological reflection. (2011, 122)

Kidner calls the author "an explorer" who is groping for the truth (1976, 13). In his explorations, he is not afraid to push boundaries and ask difficult questions that sometimes make us uncomfortable.

Towner says we will be disappointed if we expect the book to help us better understand God, as most other OT books do. It is not about God. Ecclesiastes is a book of "ideas" on how a follower of God can survive in a world that is confused and confusing (Towner 1997, 283). As such, its purpose is similar to Proverbs, which also attempts to help people live successfully in a mixed-up world. Like Proverbs, it has a positive word of advice: "By taking charge of what they can in their lives, human beings can find joy and happiness" (284). As in Proverbs, the choice is ours to make—whether to seek and accept the enjoyment that God makes available or to follow the foolish inclinations of our own heart. This message is found throughout the Bible.

Davis, like Towner, commends Qohelet for focusing our attention on the human condition (2000, 169). Qohelet knows better than anyone else in the OT what it means to be human with all of its limitations (including death). Unless we recognize our limitations and align our lives to live within them, we will never understand what it means to live successfully and with real joy in our hearts. Davis then shows how this concept relates to the Christian faith:

> It is because of the very earthiness of Koheleth's religious vision that his book serves an important function as a kind of preface to the New Testament, as some Christians have long seen. He

keeps us from hearing the gospel as a fairy tale about a fantasy world where we might be free from the basic facts of life that constrain us in this present one. Reading Ecclesiastes regularly should motivate Christians to be rigorous in correlating the gospel's demand and promise with the realities of their daily experience, to treasure and give thanks for God's good gifts that we are continually receiving even in this cramped world. (2000, 169)

I have purposely included several of the more positive interpretations of Ecclesiastes. This is to show that some thoughtful contemporary scholars contend that the book has a valuable place in the biblical canon. However, we do not need to wait until recent times to find positive words about the book's value. The final editor of Ecclesiastes makes it clear that this book contains excellent knowledge from a wise sage that is worthy of our consideration (Eccles. 12:9-14). Its words are words of truth (v. 10) that complement orthodox Israelite theology. "Fear God and keep his commandments" is still "the duty of all mankind" for both Ecclesiastes and mainstream OT theology (v. 13; see 3:14; 5:7; 8:12). Even so, human curiosity arising from life's troubles will always lead us to ask difficult questions about God and the world and ourselves.

In most biblical books, we are not prone to question the views of the author. Passages such as the requirements of the covenant in Deuteronomy, the calls to repentance in the Prophets, the words of Jesus in the Gospels, and the admonitions to holy living in Paul's letters are all considered a word from the Lord. In contrast, the words of Qohelet in Ecclesiastes are different. There have been many criticisms of his views because they are so dissimilar from the other biblical books. As mentioned above, there is a wide variety of interpretations from negative to positive. In this book, I attempt to provide some of both, where appropriate. There are some places where Qohelet is definitely correct, such as his evaluation of the sad state of human society. Apparently, it was just as bad in his day as in ours. At the same time, Qohelet needs to be more accurate in his designation of the cause, that being sin. He places too much blame on God's silence resulting in human confusion. Undoubtedly, the era when he lived partially influenced his perspective—his lifetime was prior to the incarnation and the coming of Christ.

6. Sermons from Ecclesiastes May Be Able to Reach Some of the More Skeptical Members of Your Congregation

Some people in every congregation are just like Jesus's disciple Thomas. They have a hard time accepting Jesus as their Lord and Savior because they are skeptical about the Christian faith. They come to church primarily for the social benefits or because a family member insists, but they really have no personal faith in Christ. They have heard many preachers wax eloquent on the benefits of being a Christian. Yet they remain skeptical because they have seen so little of the faith lived out in people's lives. Church politics have made them cynical. Congregational power struggles, compromises made in the interests of secular politics, the moral failures of members of the clergy, and the un-Christlike behavior of some church members—all these problems and more have convinced them that Christianity is not for them.

For such people, Ecclesiastes may be a book that they can identify with. Its author was also skeptical of the Israelite faith of his day. Just like people today who have been brought up in the church but have later rejected it, Qohelet had a hard time believing the wisdom theology he had been taught while growing up. He openly points out concepts that troubled him and why he could not accept them. He raises a number of serious questions that are still relevant today. He deserves to be taken seriously.

Other people who may find a sympathetic companion in Qohelet are those who are struggling with grief, discouragement, and hopelessness. Davis remarks, "One of my students, who suffers from recurrent bouts of depression, says that reading Ecclesiastes is 'like slipping into a warm bath'" (2000, 159). So plan your sermons in a way that touches on the questions about life and faith that nonbelievers and depressed individuals are asking today. The same questions probably motivated the author of Ecclesiastes.

7. Plan to Preach a Series of Sermons from Ecclesiastes

Ecclesiastes probably has too much pessimism in it to keep a typical congregation interested for months on end. I hope that preachers can find enough material in this book to fill a month of sermons and that many readers will attempt to do that. My book contains seven sermon starters. This should give any congregation a substantial taste of how skepticism, cynicism, and realism can sometimes lead us to move beyond popular superficial perceptions about life and Christianity and seek after a deeper level of faith.

8. A Word to Teachers

I wrote these two volumes to encourage pastors to preach more sermons from Proverbs and Ecclesiastes. However, I would also like to challenge Sunday school teachers and Bible study group leaders to tackle these two wisdom books. There are many, many topics in these books that could profitably be addressed in a teacher-student format. May your faith be strengthened and your knowledge increased as you seek to uncover some of the Bible's best instructions on successful living.

I. SUPERSCRIPTION (ECCLES. 1:1)

Introductory Sermon (Eccles. 1:1)

An introductory sermon to a series on Ecclesiastes requires special attention. This book is so different from the other books in the OT that the congregation needs to be prepared from the start. One way to begin is to highlight some of the verses in the book that are already familiar to churchgoers. Most people are familiar with its pessimistic comments about life at the beginning of the book: "Vanity of vanities! All is vanity" (Eccles. 1:2, NRSV). Another well-known verse speaks to the continual recurrence of the same types of events: "There is nothing new under the sun" (v. 9). A third passage deals with the author's thoughts about time: "There is a time for everything, and a season for every activity under the heavens: a time to be born and a time to die, a time to plant and a time to uproot, . . ." (3:1-8). People may not be as familiar with the favorite verse of all college students: "Much study is a weariness of the flesh" (12:12, NRSV).

However, some of these passages have not always been interpreted well. So one of the goals of any series of sermons from Ecclesiastes is to provide a sound interpretation of the book and practical applications for modern congregations. Let's begin with some basic information about the book and its author.

1. The Author Was an Israelite Wisdom Teacher (a Sage)

An important topic in an introductory sermon is to elucidate as much as we can know about the author of the book. Many interpreters, for lack of a better designation, refer to the author as Qohelet (*qōhelet*, pronounced ko-hell-et), meaning "gatherer." This designation appears in Ecclesiastes 1:1-2, 12; 7:27; 12:8-10. This is probably not a personal name. In 12:8 and the emended form of 7:27 a definite article, *"the* Gatherer," is placed before it (AT). This probably indicates that Qohelet is actually a title of respect the author gained through his work. He became known as a teacher who *gathered* students into his home or classroom to teach them wisdom sayings and guide their thinking about the meaning of life.

Qohelet, however, went about his teaching in a different way than most sages. He was uncomfortable with many of their beliefs and assumptions. He could not accept the happy mindset of the sages who produced Proverbs. Life was just too mixed-up and confusing to be happy about it. For this reason, the book of Ecclesiastes he produced is mostly pessimistic in tone. In the latter part of the book, he shared some positive ideas about how to cope and even experience joy in a confusing world.

There was also another person involved in the production of Ecclesiastes. An editor added the first verse (Eccles. 1:1) as an introduction and the final six verses of the book as an epilogue (12:9-14). These verses are written in the third person rather than the first person, which appears in the main part of the book. This has raised scholarly questions about the editor's purpose and viewpoint. Did the editor agree with Qohelet's teachings and simply want to present them to the world? (We find a similar situation in King Lemuel's presentation of his mother's teachings in Prov. 31:1-9.) Or did the editor disagree with Qohelet's theology and add the epilogue as a warning to readers to approach this book with caution? Some scholars suggest that the editor simply used Qohelet's words as "a foil, a teaching device" to advance his own agenda in the epilogue (Longman 1998, 38). Others believe Qohelet never existed. He is a fictional persona, and the teachings attributed to him are a creation of the editor (Fox 2004, x).

I take the position that Qohelet was a real wisdom teacher who attracted students and challenged them with his teachings. The major part of the book is a collection of his lectures and observations about life. Whether he intended the book to be circulated is unknown. Later, one of his students or friends edited the book into its final form—adding the introductory verse and the concluding epilogue to give readers some information about the author and a stamp of approval. Certainly, the editor recognized that Qohelet's teachings were difficult to hear, but at the same time, the editor thought that people needed to learn them. By publishing the thorny book of Ecclesiastes, the editor acknowledged that life was not nearly as rosy as Proverbs seemed to imply.

The other phrases in Ecclesiastes 1:1 ("son of David" and "king in Jerusalem") were added by the final editor to associate the book with Solomon. In the books of Samuel and Kings, of course, David had no son named Qohelet. The only sons of David who ever served as king were Absalom, who served only briefly as a usurper (2 Sam. 15–18), and his legitimate heir to the throne, Solomon. These phrases were probably intended to lend Solomon's authority to the book as did Proverbs 1:1. The editor, following the author's lead (Eccles. 1:12), wanted the readers of the book to think this is what Solomon would have thought about these topics had he been asked.

Even though we do not know the author's given name, there are several of his characteristics that we can discover from verses scattered throughout the book.

- The author was a sage praised by his students and other sages as wise, studious, knowledgeable, and truthful (12:9-10). He conducted research into the meaning of life using proverbial sayings and human experience. He acted much like a professor (Kidner 1976, 13).
- He was a creative writer. No other book in the Bible or in ANE literature is quite like it.
- He uses a late form of the Hebrew language with a strong influence from Aramaic.
- There are two Persian loanwords in his book. This suggests that he probably lived after the exile in the fifth or fourth centuries BC, when the Jews were a part of the Persian Empire and Aramaic was the spoken language.
- He was probably an old man, for he looks back to earlier days when life was more pleasant for him (12:1-8).
- He was probably childless, for he does not know what will happen to his estate when he dies (2:18-21; 4:8; 5:10; 6:2).

2. The Book Is a Part of the Wisdom Literature

Ecclesiastes belongs with Proverbs, Job, and Song of Songs as one of the OT's wisdom books. Its form is that of a longer, reflective book about the meaning of life. Wisdom literature was known throughout the ANE from as early as 2000 BC. Many wisdom books were written in the form of narratives about individuals who came on hard times and struggled to make sense of why this happened. Job follows this pattern.

Ecclesiastes is different because it has no storyline. It straightforwardly questions the meaning of life resulting from the author's personal observations gathered over many years. These observations convinced him that the ultimate meaning of life is unknowable. Life has its good times, but there are also many bad times. All around us we see corruption, injustice, dishonesty, conflicts, inconsistencies, betrayals, and especially death. Additionally, the sad part is that we cannot do anything about these challenges or prepare for them, because their occurrences are unpredictable. Therefore, life for human beings is senseless. There is no hope that we will ever understand it or improve our condition in any way. Qohelet's approach is that of a Socrates who will not let us escape the difficult questions of life, even though we do not want to face them. His words are like "goads" (Eccles. 12:11) that prod us into examining our knowledge of God, of our world, and of ourselves.

3. The Structure of the Book Is Based on Its Collections

Ecclesiastes contains a number of small units of thought that have no logical arrangement. Some have suggested that these units were the main topics of his face-to-face teachings. They are like "a notebook of ideas by a philosopher/theologian about the downside and upside of life" (Towner 1997, 278). They very well may be. However, scholars are not sure about the number of topics on which he intended to lecture. Some propose that there were as few as three to five divisions in the book. Others have identified as many as fifty. Most have a number somewhere in the teens or twenties. My outline includes fifteen:

1:1	Superscription
1:2-11	Theme and Repetitive Acts That Illustrate the Theme
1:12–2:26	Three Experiments
3:1-22	A Time for Everything

My favorite comment on the organization of the book is a quote by Anderson: Ecclesiastes is "a rambling lecture on the meaning of life given by a professional wisdom teacher" (1986, 583). In other words, we have clear evidence of the first absent-minded professor in history.

Even though the structure of the book is disorganized, it does show considerable creativity in its literary forms. There are short observations, instructions, rhetorical questions, numerical sayings, better-than sayings, beatitudes, woe sayings, and emblematic comparisons. This indicates that the author was well educated, but the source of his education is unknown.

4. The Tone of the Book Is Personal and Skeptical

The sages who produced the book of Proverbs were positive about life. They were confident that their views were correct and that their advice would lead to a blessed life. They claimed that this was the way God wanted humans to live.

The author of Ecclesiastes had none of their confidence. His observations had left him skeptical of any traditional answers and clichés. He was also skeptical of the prophets' claim to speak for God ("Thus says the Lord"). How could anyone know the mind of God? He had no time for priests and religious leaders associated with the temple. He only mentions the covenant, the temple, and the sacrificial system in one place (Eccles. 5:1-7). He viewed God as quite distant from human beings. Qohelet believed we cannot know God personally or comprehend his plans for the world. Despite that, we can still live lives that experience happiness.

Qohelet wanted his readers to think about the overall meaning of life using everyday experiences to illustrate valid conclusions. He offered himself as their guide, sharing with his readers what he had observed in life and what he had learned from his observations. This was very personal for him. He never appealed to any authority other than himself. He was like a scientist who had conducted his own personal experiments. These had led him to conclusions he was willing to share with his students. He was not troubled by the skeptical, even cynical nature of his teachings. The truth was more important to him than making people like him.

5. Be Prepared for a Vigorous Debate

Reading Ecclesiastes is like facing a skilled debater who will challenge your most cherished beliefs. His purpose was to raise serious issues about life that many people do not want to face. He did not attack readers personally and call into question their character, like many politicians do today. Nor did he deride their background or lack of education. He just wanted readers to face the reality of human existence. He wanted to know where they found meaning in life, especially in light of the obvious injustice, corruption, depravity, heartache, confusion, and inconsistency in the world.

Have you thought seriously about your purpose in life and where you are headed? Have you considered what your world is like? Have you talked to God about his intentions for you? And have you gotten some good answers in reply?

Many people have not done any serious thinking about these issues. They just live day after day on the surface of life and have never dived into the depths. Qohelet wanted his readers to be sadder, but wiser (to cite a modern proverb).

Strap yourself in. We are going on a mental roller-coaster ride. There will be ups and downs, sharp turns to the right and to the left, and even some loop-the-loops when our minds are turned upside down.

The question we all need to ask as we begin a study of Ecclesiastes is, How honest are we going to be as we try to answer Qohelet's probing questions? Are we willing to face the truth of his pointed observations about the meaning of life? Or will we hide behind our self-created masks and just dismiss him as a troubled, supercynical, skeptical eccentric? The answer that we give will determine the usefulness of this biblical book in our own lives.

Possible Sermon Titles: "Meet the Bible's Skeptic," "The Socrates of the Bible," "A Wise Person's Struggle with Life," "Are You Struggling to Find Meaning in Life?" "Wisdom Requires Looking Deeper Than Surface Perceptions," "A Word from a Skeptical Sage," "And You Thought You Were Cynical"

II. THEME AND REPETITIVE ACTS THAT ILLUSTRATE THE THEME (ECCLES. 1:2-11)

Vanity of Vanities (Eccles. 1:2-11)

Have you ever had a bad hair day? Probably most of us have. On at least one really bad hair day, nothing could make our hair look right. The same thing can happen with life's circumstances. We can have a "terrible, horrible, no good, very bad day" (after "Alexander" in Judith Viorst's 1972 children's story). It may have been so bad that we even wished, like Job, that that day had been taken out of the calendar so that we would not have had to experience its events (Job 3:6). There have been times when our world, our family, our hopes, and even our faith have collapsed around us and left us feeling empty and confused, even angry at life. Sometimes nothing makes sense. Life can seem to be at a dead end with no way forward.

Have you ever experienced a bad hair year or even a bad hair *lifespan*? Ecclesiastes 1:2-11 introduces us to one man's description of his bad hair life.

We do not know his real name, but he was called Qohelet. This Hebrew name means "the Gatherer." (The NIV and the NRSV translate the word as "the Teacher"; the KJV consistently translates this term as "the Preacher.") Apparently, he was a well-known wisdom teacher who gathered students together and taught them in the ways of wisdom using all kinds of collected wisdom sayings as the basis of his teachings.

For centuries, "vanity" (KJV) has been the generally accepted English translation of the key word in Qohelet's teachings. The Hebrew word *hebel* (pronounced he-vel; Eccles. 1:2) appears thirty-eight times in Ecclesiastes. This remarkable frequency suggests that Qohelet used it repeatedly in his classroom.

Commentators disagree about whether Qohelet himself wrote 1:2, as I think he did. It may, however, have come from the hand of the editor. In either case, *hebel* is the clear theme of the book, so it rightly belongs at the beginning. Qohelet uses it like a trumpet blast to grab our attention with this emotionally charged claim.

The basic meaning of *hebel* is "breath" or "vapor," but it has that meaning only a few times in the OT (e.g., Prov. 21:6). Most often it serves as a metaphor for something (1) *without substance* (shallow, superficial, empty, cannot be grasped physically); (2) *short lived* (transitory, fleeting, ephemeral); (3) *without value* (worthless, meaningless, futile); or (4) *"counter-rational"* (Fox 2004, xix) (senseless, incomprehensible, absurd, contrary to reason or common sense, cannot be grasped mentally).

Certainty about the correct translation in Ecclesiastes 1:2 is complicated because there is no context to aid us. It is just a blanket observation that everything in life is *hebel*. Further, the entire context of Ecclesiastes is no help because the word seems to use all four meanings in its thirty-eight occurrences. In the four versions I consulted, translators used four different translations, all supporting the third meaning—something without value: "meaningless" (NIV), "vanity" (NRSV), "useless" (GNT), and "futile" (NJPS). However, since 1:2 is the theme verse for the entire book, we probably should include all four meanings in our interpretation. Life is like a vapor—it lacks substance, it is short lived, it is without value, and it is utterly senseless. This is "the sum total" of life according to Qohelet (Kidner 1976, 22).

Note that Qohelet not only applied this word to life but also did so in a most extreme way. He used the phrase "vanity of vanities" (NRSV). This is a Hebrew superlative: "the greatest vanity of all vanities," "vanity to the highest degree," or "the mother of all vanities." Brown calls it "a vanity of cosmic proportion" (2011, 21). This is comparable to the title "Song of Songs," which refers to the greatest song of all songs, and the "holy of holies," namely, the holiest of all holy places in the temple.

Qohelet used this phrase to express his extreme frustration about life. Life seemed to lack any sense of meaning. His rhetorical question in Ecclesiastes 1:3 forces readers to think about the value of their own endeavors in life: "What do people gain from all their labors at which they toil under the sun?" In effect, he is asking each of us, "What is the purpose of all your efforts in life—your schooling, work, marriage, raising a family, social interactions, hobbies, entertainment, and so forth? Have you gained any value, any benefits, or any advantages from participating in these activities? What do you have to show for all your work and activities? Is there some achievement of which to be proud? Or do your activities simply fill up the time between birth and death?" Qohelet thought most of our activities are just time fillers. Like hamsters on a treadmill, our busy lives get us nowhere.

Qohelet answered his own question in 2:11: "Then my thoughts turned to all the fortune my hands had built up, to the wealth I had acquired and won—and oh, it was all futile and pursuit of wind; there was no real value under the sun!" (NJPS). In other words, all *his* life's work was of no value. But Qohelet wants you to answer the question for yourself.

Qohelet told us why he asked this question in 1:4-11. He had observed many activities taking place in nature, but nothing ever seemed to change permanently. The sun rises in the morning and makes its way across the sky, but the next morning it returns to the same place and repeats the same journey. Likewise, the wind blows from one direction and then another, but it never seems to be going anywhere. It just spirals around to where it started and begins over again. Streams also have this repetitive pattern of motion. They originate in the mountains and flow downhill into the sea, but the sea never rises or overflows its shoreline. In the end, the water never accomplishes its mission. Its activity is for naught. Qohelet's examples prove his point that there are endless cycles of activity in nature, yet the earth never changes. There is plenty of motion, but nothing new ever occurs: "What has been will be again, what has been done will be done again; there is nothing new under the sun" (v. 9).

Many of us would like to argue with Qohelet's point here. "What about all the new discoveries and changes in technology, astronomy, biology, communication, and transportation?" we ask. "Scientists are discovering new things all the time." No doubt Qohelet would have answered, "Are they really new or just newly discovered by human beings? God has known about them since the beginning of time."

Qohelet noted that he observed the same repetitious pattern in the lives of human beings. When one generation of people comes to an end, they seem to have made excellent gains. Yet when they die, life seems to revert back to its original state. The new generation does not remember the former ones or their accomplishments (v. 11). Thus they repeat the same activities and make the same mistakes as the previous generations before them. These same repetitious activities will continue forever into the future. Qohelet wanted to know why we have not learned anything new about how to make things better permanently.

If Qohelet were here today, he would probably ask us questions such as, Why do we still have poverty? Why is there still greed? Why is there still corruption in governments? Why are there still dysfunctional families? Why is there still war? Shouldn't one World War have been enough to convince humanity that countries should never go to war again? How can there still be leaders who can justify sending thousands of young men to their deaths to take the territory of another sovereign nation?

For Qohelet, the world just continues on and on with no significant progress from any one generation. It is like streams that continually flow into the sea without any visible changes to the sea. Generations of human beings live and die without leaving any evidence of having improved society. They might as well have never lived because they leave no lasting legacy.

Qohelet's cynical view of life made an important point. Much of life is routine and repetitious. I eat three times a day and sleep every night. I try to spend a little time every day on writing projects. Once a week I mow the lawn, put the trash out, and help my wife with the grocery shopping. Several times a month I pay our bills as they appear in our mailbox. Once a year I get a physical exam and visit my dentist and ophthalmologist. There is continual activity in my life, but is there any purpose to it? Or is it just an unending cycle of repetitious events? This is what Qohelet was trying to get us to consider.

Further, according to Qohelet, we cannot understand God's purposes in all of this repetitive activity, since he does not tell us (5:2 [5:1 HB]). We are in the dark about the ultimate meaning of life, and we are all headed toward Sheol/death, which may happen at any time (8:8; 9:12). Our life's work will then come to an end, and our estate will pass to someone else (2:18-21). It is all senseless and meaningless. Life is nothing more than total vanity.

We should not be surprised at Qohelet's skepticism. One obvious purpose of the book is to raise questions about generally accepted beliefs and force readers to think deeply about the meaning of life. Moreover, it is framed in a short, catchy way that could be placed on a bumper sticker: "Vanity of vanities! All is vanity" (v. 2, NRSV).

We should note that Qohelet was not the only biblical writer to describe life as vanity—fleeting and meaningless. The psalmist, too, made note of the human condition (Pss. 8:3-4 [4-5 HB]; 39:5-6, 11 [6-7, 12 HB]; 62:9 [10 HB]; 94:11; 144:3-4). The author of Job did as well (Job 7:1-10, 16; 9:29).

Perhaps Qohelet meant something like this. We all live most of our days on the surface of life. We fill our time on earth with working, eating, sleeping, conversing, shopping, cleaning, mowing, being entertained, and so forth. These activities have become so habitual that sometimes we cannot even remember that they happened. Before we know it, a whole year of days has gone by and we are one year older and closer to death. The only things that interrupt this steady rhythm of life are major crises, such as a serious car accident, a diagnosis of cancer, the death of a family member, or a major national event like September 11, 2001, in the United States or the 2016 Berlin Christmas market truck attack in Germany. Even then, many people only pause briefly to reflect. In a few days, they are back to the same activities as before. They never ask any significant questions about life.

Was Qohelet's examination of human life correct? Is this *all* that can be said about this topic? The answer is no. We know the practical way to distinguish a pessimist from an optimist: Show them both a glass of water and ask them to describe it. Is it half-full or half-empty?

Qohelet would have said it is half-empty, but many others in the Bible would say it is half-full.

For example, in Ecclesiastes 1:5, Qohelet described the repetitive and wearisome task of the sun, which must rise and set each day. His description sounds as if the sun would rather not shine anymore. On the contrary, the psalmist compared the sun to a bridegroom, eager to traverse the heavens each day and share its warmth with the world (Ps. 19:4-6 [5-7 HB]). It is the same sun that is being described, but one view is from a pessimist and the other from an optimist.

Here are others in the Bible whose view of life is much more optimistic than Qohelet's. First, Qohelet's view of life was totally at odds with the viewpoint of the sages in Proverbs. For these authors, there were definite rewards to be gained from our labors, if we fear God and live a life of wisdom. God would bless our efforts abundantly with long life, prosperity, well-being, and so forth (see the sermon "Wisdom's Rewards" in Bowes 2025, 51, as well as Prov. 2–3; 12:11; 14:23).

Second, Qohelet's view of life was also at odds with the teachings of Moses. Moses urged the Israelites to think back and relive the experiences of their past. He continually warned them that they would be forced to repeat the mistakes of previous generations if they failed to remember what God had taught them in the past. They should never forget what God had delivered them from in Egypt (Deut. 5:15). They should never forget what God had taught them at Mount Sinai (4:5-14). They should never forget what God had done for them in getting them through the wilderness (8:2-5). Remembering and acting on those memories allows us to move on to new experiences in the future.

Today, both Jews and Christians find Qohelet's views about the vanity of life to be lacking. He was too nearsighted. His vision did not extend far enough. Jews look to the long history of God's providential care and his promises through the covenant. Christians find hope in Christ's resurrection, his forgiveness of sins, and his promise of eternal life. There are other ways of looking at the world besides Qohelet's. This should be a great encouragement to all of us.

It is interesting that the NT never quotes from the book of Ecclesiastes. We should not be surprised. However, Paul alluded to Ecclesiastes 1:2 in Romans 8:19-21. There Paul used the word "frustration" (*mataioteti*) rather than "vanity" to describe the present state of the natural world. Nature is "cursed as a consequence of Adam's sin (Gen 3:17)" (Greathouse with Lyons 2008, 261). God has subjected it to emptiness/meaninglessness.

Romans differs from Ecclesiastes in three ways. First, it applies meaninglessness only to the natural world instead of humanity. Second, it lays the blame for this meaninglessness on human sin, rather than God's hidden purposes. Third, it offers hope for the removal of this meaninglessness through Christ's resurrection and the redemption of our bodies at his second coming. By this means, Paul provided the Christian answer to Qohelet's pessimism about the vanity of life.

Finally, there are other ways of looking at the repetitive patterns of nature and society besides Qohelet's. The regularity of nature teaches us about the stability and reliability of God. His plans for the earth include predictable patterns we can depend on to order our lives. They are clear examples of God's gracious governance of the world. The sun, the wind, and the water are all essential to human survival. Without their regularity, we would not exist. Qohelet would want us to acknowledge that and to thank God for these gifts.

Our "bad hair days" can be put to good use. As we grow older and have the opportunity to look back over the years, we sometimes discover that God used such days to teach us some important lessons about life we might never have learned any other way. We do not like to dwell on our bad days. They are too depressing, but they can make us grateful for the routine and repetition of ordinary days.

What will be your perspective on life? Will it be pessimistic and cynically limited like Qohelet's? Or will it be optimistic and full of gratitude for all God has done through creation, the incarnation, the resurrection, and redemption? Will we complain about the monotony of life or testify to God's daily care and involvement in our lives, even in difficult times? As other Scriptures teach us, life does not have to be a "vanity of vanities." Will your glass be half-full or half-empty?

Possible Sermon Titles: "A Really Bad Hair Day," "Is 'Vanity' the Last Word on Life's Meaning?" "What Does It Profit?" "So Where Do You Find Meaning in Life?" "The Absurdity of Life"

III. THREE EXPERIMENTS (ECCLES. 1:12–2:26)

The Search for Meaning in Life (Eccles. 1:12–2:26)

For over one hundred years, physicists have tried to create a unified theory of the interaction between all the known, fundamental forces and particles in the universe. Albert Einstein was the best-known of these physicists, but many others have contributed or are still contributing to the research on this topic. Enormous strides have been made, but so far, scientists have not succeeded in creating a "theory of everything."

In Ecclesiastes 1:12–2:26, Qohelet described his own attempts to create a similar type of theory. Only, instead of investigating the natural world as physicists do, he researched the various ways people try to find meaning in life. Is there one unified theory that explains the best way to live in relationship to God, to the world around us, and to others?

To answer this question, Qohelet took on the persona of a king (1:12)—he impersonated Solomon. Solomon had the reputation of being the wisest and wealthiest Israelite who ever lived—as wealthy as any billionaire today. He had the means to conduct whatever experiments interested him. Nothing could prevent him from getting to the heart of any question about life. If someone like Solomon could not find a good answer to this inquiry, then no one could.

For a long time, scholars have debated why Qohelet did not just come out and say he was impersonating Solomon. We do not know. However, taking on the guise of some distinguished personality of the past was a common "literary device" used in ancient literature to bolster its authority (Gordis 1968, 76). Numerous examples are found in the intertestamental literature known as the Apocrypha and Pseudepigrapha (e.g., Baruch, Epistle of Jeremiah, Wisdom of Solomon, *Testament of Abraham*, and *Testament of Moses*). None of these books were actually written by the person in the title.

Qohelet chose Solomon because Solomon was a well-known authority on the topics Qohelet wanted to discuss. From an Israelite perspective, no one could top Solomon in wisdom, wealth, pleasure, and folly. He had sought and experienced all of them to the extreme. He would be an ideal authority to share his ideas about whether they contributed to understanding the meaning of life. His views would carry substantial weight in the minds of most Israelites. Perhaps, Qohelet chose Solomon to counter the skeptical tone of his book. Otherwise, some readers might have rejected his book as just the crazy ideas of a "lonely rebel" (Rad 1972, 235). He needed the support of a kindred spirit, a well-respected authority figure in the wisdom community.

The project Qohelet proposed was massive—to investigate *all* aspects of the world ("all that is done under the heavens" [1:13]), with the goal of finding the real meaning of life. The tools he used were (1) observations and (2) rational thinking skills. In today's vernacular, we would say that he used the same kinds of problem-solving skills that children learn in school every day.

1. Qohelet's First Experiment: Wisdom (Eccles. 1:12-18)

Qohelet, in the guise of Solomon, conducted three experiments in his search for the meaning of life. His first experiment was to devote himself to gaining as much wisdom as possible. He does not tell us what activities he engaged in or for how long he carried out the experiment. These verses apparently intended to get the attention of any sages who might read his book. He had studied the same books they had, such as collections of proverbs and wisdom instructions about life. He had disciplined himself, as all wise people do, by rejecting the practices condemned in the book of Proverbs—folly, laziness, drunkenness, carousing with loose women, dishonesty, and all types of evil speech. Instead, he had engaged in practices that are praised in Proverbs—fearing God, obeying one's parents, following the advice of Lady Wisdom, being a good friend and neighbor, and guarding his speech.

The results of his first experiment were extremely frustrating. He called this experiment "an unhappy business" (Eccles. 1:13, NRSV). It was unhappy for several reasons.

First, his investigations led him to discover that God is extremely transcendent (5:2 [5:1 HB]). He lives in heaven and does not communicate well or often with human beings. He keeps many things to himself. Therefore, we are in the dark about many questions we would like answered.

Qohelet was frustrated that God made human beings curious about the meaning of life but had prevented them from ever discovering it. Trying to find the meaning of life is like "chasing after the wind" (1:14, 17). You can feel it, so you know it's there, but you can never catch it. This is the frustrating predicament that we find ourselves in. Will we ever know what our existence means?

Second, gaining wisdom was unhappy for Qohelet because God has created the world in such a way that some things cannot be changed. He used a proverb to drive home his point: "What is crooked ["bent/twisted," not "corrupt"] cannot be straightened" (v. 15).

God controls the world and determines its overall direction. Whatever inconsistencies and injustices may exist in the world are ultimately God's responsibility. Job agreed with Qohelet on this point (Job 9:1-24; 12:7-25; 19:6-20; 21:6-26). Qohelet wanted to use his hard-acquired wisdom to make the world a better place. He wanted to change some things that seemed wrong, unjust, or inconsistent to him. He wanted to add some things he thought were missing. But God's sovereignty over creation prevented him from doing so. "What greater pain is there than to have the ability and insight to change things, but to live without the possibility of doing so?" (Horne 2003, 399).

Third, the more Qohelet attempted to live a life of wisdom, the more disillusioned he became. His pursuit of wisdom had made him increasingly knowledgeable about how life operates and what needs to be changed. Yet his knowledge had not enlightened him on life's overall meaning. It had only filled him with "sorrow" and "grief" for all that was wrong with the world (Eccles. 1:18). This made no sense to him. He concluded that life was nothing more than vanity (v. 14).

Qohelet's statement in verse 18 needs further comment. If increased wisdom and knowledge only brings increased disillusionment, then why do we send our children to school? We are only setting them up for discouragement and failure. In one sense, Qohelet is right. Increased knowledge does reveal how much more knowledge we lack. Because of the explosion of knowledge in the past century, today no one can ever master even one field of knowledge, much less all fields. That is discouraging.

But Qohelet was not speaking of the knowledge we gain in school to understand nature or earn a living or be good citizens. He was speaking of the knowledge needed to comprehend the overall meaning of life. For him, life is basically not understandable, and it has always been so. God created the world this way, and he refuses to make it sensible to human beings. Thus gaining more knowledge and wisdom cannot help us understand life. It can only make us more frustrated and disillusioned.

Qohelet's first experiment had failed. His pursuit of wisdom had not satisfied his longing for a meaningful understanding of life. One might expect him to abandon wisdom altogether. However, he could not bring himself to do that, for wisdom was ingrained in his psyche. He would put wisdom aside for the moment, but he would come back to its value later (2:12-18; 7:11-12, 19; 9:13-18).

2. Qohelet's Second Experiment: Pleasure (Eccles. 2:1-11)

Qohelet's second experiment was at the opposite extreme from wisdom. He sought to fill his life with as many pleasures as he could indulge in. He engaged in activities that brought him contentment and laughter. He drank wine. He built houses, gardens, parks, and reservoirs. He planted fruit trees. He acquired large herds of farm animals. He bought numerous slaves to manage his property. He possessed large amounts of silver and gold—the expected marks of a great king. For his parties, he hired skilled entertainers. One further pleasure was his large harem of women. According to 1 Kings 11:3, Solomon had seven hundred wives and three hundred concubines. There was simply no pleasure that he did not try (Eccles. 2:10; see the historian's description of Solomon's luxurious lifestyle in 1 Kings 4:20-34).

Modern readers should expect to be offended by Qohelet's exploitation of human beings in his experience of pleasure. But unfortunately, slavery and royal harems were a part of the social world of ancient times.

Qohelet tells us that he worked hard to gain these pleasures, and he enjoyed achieving them. In the process, he acquired a reputation as the greatest king who had ever ruled in Jerusalem (Eccles. 2:9). No doubt he accomplished much in his experiment. But alas, it was all self-centered. Commentators repeatedly point out the multiple times that first-person singular verbs appear in this passage: "I did this" or "I did that." Qohelet was totally obsessed with himself. He denied himself nothing (v. 10).

Qohelet's pursuit of pleasure brought him no satisfaction. He was just as frustrated and confused as before. What had he gained? More fun? More self-gratification? Undoubtedly! Yet a deep understanding of life was missing. The increase in his physical pleasure and wealth was all senseless to him. Life was still "meaningless, a chasing after the wind" (v. 11). Qohelet's second experiment was also a failure.

Qohelet failed to mention that the pursuit of pleasure was a lot more popular than the pursuit of wisdom, but we know this to be the case. Witness the number of people who buy lottery tickets hoping to be able to quit their jobs and live happily ever after. Apparently, they had never read Qohelet's negative evaluation of the life of pleasure or Jesus's parable of the rich fool (Luke 12:13-21).

3. Qohelet's Third Experiment: A Comparison of Wisdom and Folly (Eccles. 2:12-16)

For his third experiment, Qohelet chose to make a comparison between wisdom and folly. His first experiment proved that wisdom was not all it was cracked up to be (Eccles. 1:16-18). But maybe it had some inherent advantages that make it more valuable than the pathway of the fool.

What he found surprised him. The sages were right, but only up to a point. In the present moment, seeking to live by wisdom is much, much better than pursuing folly. It is like light in comparison to darkness (2:13). However, in the overall scheme of things, it really has no lasting advantage.

There is no reward for wisdom in the long run, because both wise people and fools will die and quickly be forgotten. As with Cinderella, the clock will strike midnight for all of us, and we will be snatched away to another existence. Therefore, why should we exert ourselves to be wise when we are going to die anyway? You will then go to Sheol—the OT designation for the place of the dead (see Bowes 2018, 86-87, for a description of Sheol). In death, the wise are no better off than the fools. The fate of both is the same.

Qohelet seems to have been terribly angry at this. He felt the sages had deceived him and everyone else by praising the life of wisdom. But it was no better than the life of folly. Should there not be some advantage for the wise person, like living longer or forever? For Qohelet, this thought proved his conclusion that life makes no sense. No one can understand it, and no one will ever understand it, unless God chooses to tell us. Qohelet's third experiment was as futile as his first two.

4. All My Life Has Been in Vain (Eccles. 2:17-23)

Qohelet's anger over his failed experiments concluded with the outburst: "So I hated life" (Eccles. 2:17). This has been the cry many people overwhelmed by the circumstances of life have voiced. It seems especially bitter coming from one who honestly tried to make sense of life and failed. From Qohelet's perspective, the failure was not due to his own inadequacies or misguided efforts. It was from God's creation of a world, which Qohelet came to see as absurd and incomprehensible. This left him without hope and joyless.

Two additional realities only added to Qohelet's anger. First, he would have to leave all his possessions to someone else when he died. That seemed very unfair and stupid to him. Why toil so hard while one is alive only to have to abandon the fruits of one's labors at death? Surely, there should be some enduring reward for our efforts in life. If not, our entire life's work is in vain. It makes no difference to God or anyone else that we ever lived.

Second, Qohelet's anger increased when he thought about those who would take over his possessions when he died. What would they do with them? Would they work as hard as he had to improve his land and possessions? Qohelet feared the worst: They would probably not appreciate their inheritance, because they did not have to work for it. They would foolishly waste it on personal pleasures.

Ironically, Solomon's heirs certainly did what Qohelet feared. Solomon was right to be worried about those who would inherit his estate and his position as king. His son Rehoboam proved to be inept and foolish, causing the division of Israel into two nations.

This plausible future made Qohelet so upset that he could not sleep at night (v. 23). His mind raced from one negative thought to another. This passage makes some suspect that Qohelet was an older man who had no wife or children to take possession of his estate when he died. He did not know who would receive his possessions or what they would do with them.

As to Qohelet's anger over the future distribution of his estate, we should note that God does not hold us accountable for how our heirs utilize our possessions. We are responsible only for what we do with them ourselves during our lifetimes. With God's help and guidance we can discern how to use them for God's glory. Parents who are excessively worried about how their estate will be treated after their death always have the legal means through wills and trusts to make sure that their estate is put to good use and distributed as they desire.

5. Joy Is Found in the Simple Things of Life (Eccles. 2:24-26)

Qohelet's thoughts take an abrupt turn in Ecclesiastes 2:24. Every comment about his experiments up to this point has emphasized the absurdity of pursuing one of the main pathways of life—wisdom, pleasure, or folly. None of them provide humans with any satisfaction. They are all meaningless.

However, Qohelet was not ready to give up entirely on life. He was not thinking about ending his life in suicide. Nor was he complaining like Job (Job 3) that he had ever been born. He was simply overwhelmed by the lack of meaning that he saw around him. Nothing in life gave him hope for the future.

This passage should point readers to an approach to life that will help them navigate the senseless parts of life. Here, Qohelet focused on the basic necessities of life—food, drink, and work (Eccles. 2:24). These were the simple things he had always enjoyed. God's prevenient grace provided him with all he needed, every day, as he had need.

When it is fairly certain that our basic needs will be met, it is easy not to think about them during an average day. We tend to assume that there will always be food and drink on our table and some kind of work for us to earn a living. When a crisis comes, or uncertainties arise (the current situation of millions in today's world), our attention is driven back to our basic physical needs, and we suddenly realize how gracious God has been to us. He is a vital part of our survival.

Here, Qohelet put aside the daunting, philosophical questions he wrestled with earlier and reverted to the basic, essential parts of life. Our physical survival absolutely depends on God's daily provision. We will not be able to think big thoughts about life if we are not adequately nourished and gainfully employed. A recognition of this should call for thanks and appreciation to the God who takes care of his people.

Qohelet was still depressed over his failure to find the ultimate meaning of life through his three experiments. But he was ready to go on living, thanking God each day for providing for his basic needs.

6. What Can Qohelet Teach Us about How to Live Our Lives Today?

Here are two lessons that we can learn from this amazing passage. First, Qohelet is a great example of the kind of serious effort we all should be making to find the real meaning of life. Some people live their entire lives without ever entertaining even one serious thought about life's purpose. They have no idea why they are here or how to act on their life's purpose. There are too many drifters, too many people who get to the end of life with nothing to show for their existence. They might as well have never lived. They leave their pastors with almost nothing to say at their funerals.

We may not be energetic enough (or have the leisure time) to conduct a series of experiments like Qohelet's. However, there needs to be a deep desire on our part to find God's plan and then live it out to the best of our ability. God will help us find his plan if we will ask.

Qohelet can definitely be commended for showing us one way to do that. Qohelet concluded that his experiments had been a failure, but we can, at least, give him credit for asking some good questions and seeking to find real meaning in life. Would that more people today would make that same effort.

Second, Qohelet described human existence as "an unhappy business" or "a chasing after the wind" or the "vanity of all vanities." God did not intend for life to be that way. The description of God's acts of creation in Genesis 1–2 reveals that God loved his creation and was extremely pleased with it. It was all good. God was especially pleased with the human beings whom he created "in his own image" (1:27).

It is true that God did not reveal everything about himself or about his world. That may frustrate those who think they have to know the "theory of everything about everything." God has given us enough information to live simply and well. And he has promised to engage with us continually through all the vanities around us. Life "should indeed be the greatest business in which God and man together can be engaged" (Atkins 1956, 32).

Most of us who are older today have become used to taking multiple pills, giving ourselves injections, and/or using medical equipment such as canes, walkers, CPAP machines, and inhalers. It is not the lifestyle we would have chosen for ourselves. We do not like the inconvenience these add to our lives. However, they are necessary to keep us alive, and they sure make a difference in how we function during the day.

In the same way, Qohelet did not like the senselessness of the world around him and the knowledge that he would lose all his possessions and achievements at his inevitable death. This was the inconvenient human condition in which he found himself. Nevertheless, he learned how to adjust his attitude and lifestyle to this reality by focusing his attention on the simple things God provided for him. They were enough to make his life worth living and give him enjoyment.

The future that lies out before us today is basically unknown and uncontrollable. That thought could be frightening and another example of life's vanities. Still, life can be enjoyed by focusing on the present, simple gifts that God has bestowed on each of us—food, drink, work, family, and friends.

This being the case, we should enjoy what we have while we have it. Our gifts are like the manna that God provided for the Israelites in the wilderness. They could not hoard it or store it up for the future, but they could enjoy it each day as it came (Farmer 1991, 153).

Possible Sermon Titles: "Qohelet the Scientist," "Three Experiments," "Three Approaches to Life," "Faith Seeking Understanding," "It's All Meaningless and Senseless," "Where Do You Find Meaning in Life?"

IV. A TIME FOR EVERYTHING (ECCLES. 3:1-22)

In His Time (Eccles. 3:1-15)

This passage is one of the most familiar in the book. It begins with a series of fourteen pairs of opposites that speak of various forms of human activity. There is some debate about the meaning of some of these matching pairs. I limit my comments to the more traditional interpretations.

- The first pair concerns the two most important events in our lives our birth and our death (Eccles. 3:2a).
- The second focuses on the seasonal activities of a farmer—planting one's field and then uprooting the dead plants in preparation for the next year's crop (v. 2b).
- The third and fourth contrast creative and destructive activities—killing and healing, tearing down and building up (v. 3).
- The fifth and sixth deal with opposite extremes of emotion and their outward display—weeping and laughing, mourning and dancing (v. 4).
- The seventh refers to scattering stones on a person's field to make it unusable versus removing stones from a field to prepare it for planting (v. 5a).
- The eighth deals with appropriate and inappropriate times to show affection (v. 5b).
- The ninth speaks of searching for something (presumably that is lost or needed) versus giving up the search (v. 6a), while the tenth refers to keeping or throwing away some of our possessions (v. 6b).

- The eleventh is probably a reference to tearing one's clothing as a part of a mourning ritual and then mending the tear after the mourning is concluded (v. 7a).
- The twelfth reiterates various sayings in Proverbs concerning the appropriate time to speak versus remaining silent (v. 7b; Prov. 10:14, 19; 11:12-13; 13:3; 15:23, 28; 17:27-28; 21:23; see the sermon "The Power of the Tongue" in Bowes 2025, 102).
- The thirteenth refers to contrasting personal attitudes that people have toward others—love and hatred (Eccles. 3:8a).
- The fourteenth broadens this thought into the interrelationships of communities and nations—war and peace (v. 8b).

This list is not comprehensive, but it includes enough different types of opposites so that Qohelet's readers would think he was referring to all possible events in life. This is confirmed by two phrases in verse 1: "a time for everything" and "a season for every activity." The author means there is an appropriate time for actions at both ends of the spectrum and for everything in between. Every event is appropriate for its time. This is not to say that the amount of time for an action at one end of the spectrum is always the same as for an action at the other end.

The word "time" ('ēt) appears in every one of the first eight verses. Qohelet did not refer to a specific month, day, and year. Rather, he meant "an occasion or situation that is *right* for something" (Fox 2004, 20). The right time is when God determines that "a certain 'need' presents itself" (Fox 1999, 206).

We might jump to the mistaken conclusion that the positive options are the better ones and that we should pursue those. But Qohelet was not suggesting we practice any of them. He merely placed before his readers a lengthy list of activities and events that may occur in life. He is saying that this is how life operates—for better or worse; each of these pairs of opposites could happen to any of us at any time.

What are we to make of this list? Commentators have suggested several interpretations. Perhaps Qohelet was emphasizing that life is about constant changes. Life is never static. Like a pendulum, it swings back and forth from one extreme to another, and it encompasses everything in between. "For every course of action in one direction, there will occur in due time an equal and opposite reaction"

(Brown 2011, 41). This is similar to Newton's third law of motion: "For every action, there is an equal and opposite reaction."

For Qohelet, there was a time for literally everything in every aspect of life (3:1). Still, the end result of all these changes is never anything new. In verse 15, we see that Qohelet thought that all the events in his list of opposites repeated themselves over and over again. Seow thinks this repetition is illustrated with the modern proverb "What goes around comes around" (1997, 169). There really is "nothing new under the sun" (1:9).

God has determined (3:14) that all of life will be similar to the repetitious movements of the sun, wind, and streams (1:4-11; → the earlier sermon "Vanity of Vanities," p. 33). They are continually on the move, but they never go anywhere new. The lesson is that humans would do well to accept the fact that life is always changing and thus unstable. We should be ready for whatever events come our way. Qohelet is right: life is always changing, but this does not seem to be the primary reason for his comments.

Another possibility is that Qohelet's views were fatalistic. Events like being born and dying (3:2) are determined by fate. When your time is up, it's up. Humans have no control over these events and cannot predict when they will happen. We sometimes hear people talk this way about a person's death: "Well, it was her time to go." But fatalism is foreign to OT theology, and it does not seem likely in Ecclesiastes. In the remaining verses in the passage (vv. 9-15), Qohelet mentions God seven times. He is the one who establishes the rhythms in life, not fate. Humans may not understand why and when things happen, but God knows about all events in his creation.

A third possibility is that God predetermines all events in life. He sets the time for people's birth and death, war and peace, and so forth. Humans are just pawns in the overall scheme of life, lacking a free will and opportunities for creativity. However, predetermination is not Qohelet's point in verse 1. His emphasis is on the *appropriateness* of every event for its time or season. Events happen at the proper time because the circumstances are right.

A much more likely interpretation is found in the wisdom theology of the sages. Here are the main points:

1. God's Order Is Found throughout All of Creation

All the sages believed that God embedded order in our universe at the time of creation. As a result, everything fits where it is supposed to fit. Life does change, and sometimes these changes are very rapid. Many times the changes of life do not make any sense to us at all. Yet overall, there is a very profound order to our world. The world was not put together haphazardly or by chance. It was established according to God's design, and it continues to operate following regular principles that can be studied and described by scientists, philosophers, and theologians. God reminded Job of this in his magnificent speech about the order of creation, the principles of divine governance, and the characteristics of each member of the animal kingdom (Job 38–41).

Invariably, I ran into problems with this concept every time I taught wisdom literature. Most of my students were glad to be in college. They were glad to be out on their own for the first time and away from the rules that their moms and dads had imposed on them at home. They went through times of discouragement and exhaustion when it got down to the end of the semester, and some talked about not returning. Usually after only a few weeks at home, they were already saying, "I want to go back to college. I like my freedom." Then in their sophomore or junior year, they ran into an OT professor of wisdom literature who told them that life is full of order and rules. God has embedded order in our universe to help us live successful lives. If we break those rules, we will end up as miserable failures. Needless to say, not every student was happy when the subject of *order* was the topic of the day.

God's order in the world, if we will acknowledge it, provides a plan for living. It identifies you and me as his children. It describes ways that we can be successful in life. It provides limits that warn us of things that would be harmful. All of these are discussed in the books of Job and Proverbs (see the sermon "Order in the Court" in Bowes 2025, 161).

Qohelet's contribution to this topic of order is to extend its application to time (Eccles. 3:1-8). There is a right time for the occurrence of every event. Wise people will recognize the truth of this and seek to adjust their lives to God's timing.

Those of us who are now older have learned the value of order, because we have experienced times of chaos. We know that we live and work best when there is order around us that provides direction, boundaries, and security.

2. God's Order Provides Suitable Times for All Activities, Including Both the Good and the Bad

When the Hebrew language gives opposites, as it does here, it intends to convey the idea of totality. It lists the bookends—"a time to be born and a time to die"—to indicate that all the experiences of life that fall between these bookends are a part of God's order for our lives. As God weaves the fabric of our lives, he incorporates all the colors of the rainbow in one place or another. Even black and white show up sometimes on our fabric.

Qohelet adds a descriptive term to the events of life. It is the word "suitable" (*yāpeh*). "[God] has made everything suitable for its time" (Eccles. 3:11, NRSV). God not only has created a time for "every activity under the heavens" (v. 1) but also has chosen a "suitable" time for its occurrence (v. 11, NRSV). The KJV and NIV use the translation "beautiful," which is appropriate in other OT passages. But here, that is not what the context calls for. It has nothing to do with aesthetics. It refers to something that is "good," "right," "proper," "appropriate."

What Qohelet claimed was that every event in his list of opposites occurred at an appropriate time. Because of our finiteness, we never see more than a small part of the past or present. That means we may never know that some events are appropriate. We may never see or understand the big picture. Yet God sees it all, and from his vantage point, everything is right for its time. Fox illustrates the appropriate time for war in this way:

> The fact that there is "a time for war" does not mean that God predestined the Congressional declaration of war against Japan on December 8, 1941. Rather, there are conditions right for war, situations when war is called for and can be effectively prosecuted. One such occasion arose immediately after the attack on Pearl Harbor. Earlier, a declaration of war would not have had popular support; later, Japan would have solidified its hold on the Pacific. (1999, 198)

This is not to say that God cannot override the appropriate time for an event such as the time for a person's death or that a person cannot speed up the time of his or her death because of foolish behavior and bad decisions (7:16-17). Jeremiah learned this lesson in his visit to the potter's house (Jer. 18:1-12). The point is that most events generally happen at suitable times within God's governance of the world. They are not predestined to happen at specific moments of time (Fox 1999, 204). God can adjust times based on human action or inaction.

Qohelet is not the only OT writer to support the idea of events occurring at suitable times. Other writers include appropriate times for the following: rain (Deut. 11:14), judgment (32:35), kings to go off to war (2 Sam. 11:1), animals to be born (Job 39:1-3), birds to migrate (Jer. 8:7), people to seek the Lord (Hos. 10:12), and rebuilding the temple (Hag. 1:2).

There are times when we all react negatively to this concept. When are earthquakes and tsunamis ever appropriate? When is cancer ever appropriate? When is death ever appropriate? The tragedies and troubles of life are *never* appropriate from our viewpoint.

Qohelet wondered about that as well. He said in Ecclesiastes 7:27-29 that he took a poll to see if anyone else understood how to make sense of life. The results of his poll were this: not one woman understood the meaning of life, and only one man out of one thousand had a good answer. Those are not very good odds, are they? Consequently, he concluded that no human being knows how these bad events fit into the big picture. It is a mystery. Only one person knows, and that is God, and he is not telling (3:10-11; 8:17).

In Genesis, we read the story of Joseph. If ever there was a person who had a right to complain, it was he. He was mistreated by his brothers, sold into slavery in Egypt, seduced by Potiphar's wife, and then thrown into jail on false charges. However, things changed for the better in Joseph's life. He rose to the position of second in command to the Pharaoh. One day his brothers stood before him shaking in fear over what he might do to them. His words to them were these: "Do not be distressed, or angry with yourselves, because you sold me here; for God sent me before you to preserve life" (Gen. 45:5, NRSV). In other words, Joseph believed that all the experiences of his life up to that point (even the bad ones) were appropriate/suitable because

God had used them to save the lives of his brothers and bring good to their large extended family. Paul echoes something similar in Romans 8:28: "And we know that in all things God works for the good of those who love him." There are other implications to this idea of suitability.

One is that we should be ready for any possibility in life because we do not know ahead of time when an appropriate occasion will occur. Thus we should be in a right relationship with God *at all times* (Pss. 16:8; 105:4; Prov. 23:17; 28:14). Jesus taught about the importance of always being ready in his parable of the ten virgins/bridesmaids (Matt. 25:1-13).

A second implication is that we should not attempt to force things to happen before their appropriate time. God is the only one who knows the right time, so patience is important (Pss. 27:14; 37:7; Gal. 5:22; Col. 3:12). David knew that God intended him to succeed Saul as Israel's king, but he refused to take matters into his own hands, waiting instead for God's time (1 Sam. 24–2 Sam. 5).

A third implication is that our failure to succeed in some endeavor is not always the result of a lack of seriousness on our part, although it may be. Rather, it could be the result of bad timing. More than one person has failed miserably at an undertaking, only to try again later and succeed. God's timing is essential for success.

Qohelet's words here raise enormous obstacles to those who believe in the gospel of success (prosperity gospel). If God has established times for both good and bad things in our lives (Eccles. 3:1; 7:14), then no amount of faith or righteousness on our part is going to protect us from *all* the bad experiences in life. Just as weeping and mourning come our way from time to time (3:4), so there will also be a time for war (v. 8) and death (v. 2). We cannot will evil and difficult times away. Neither can we earn our way out of them through overly righteous living.

When our older daughter, Heidi, was born, her uncle gave her a three-foot-tall pink, furry teddy bear with a bright green ribbon around his neck. We called him "Teddy." Like all children's toys, Teddy had a rough life. He was sat on, laid on, chewed on, spit up on, and twisted into all kinds of shapes that no bear should ever have to endure. Within three to four years, he looked pretty sad. The worst part was that he developed holes at the places where his arms and legs attached to his body. Out of those holes came hundreds of tiny, little, white Styrofoam beads that showed up everywhere in our house. I started putting pieces of tape wherever a hole developed, and soon there were so many pieces of tape that we started calling him "Patchy." My wife, Ginger, and I talked over what we ought to do. We finally decided that we would get another teddy bear and see if we could lure Heidi's affection away to another stuffed animal, and then we could dispose of Patchy.

We bought a big brown bear named "Super Bear," and we tried to encourage this new relationship. Unfortunately, it didn't work. Patchy was still her greatest object of affection. Finally, we sat down with Heidi and talked about all the messes that Patchy was making around our house. He was a nuisance and we really needed to get rid of him. She eventually agreed with us, at least mentally, that this was the logical thing to do. I was elated.

When trash day came, I put Patchy out with the other trash to be collected. We had an alley that ran down the back of our property where we placed our trash. A big fifty-five-gallon drum burn barrel was out there. I set Patchy up with his back against the burn barrel. I can still see him in my mind's eye, sitting there staring straight ahead, probably thinking about the family who had deserted him and his coming fate in a garbage truck. I went back into the house and did not see anyone, but I heard sobs coming from Heidi's bedroom. I walked down the hall to our bedroom and there was Ginger bawling away too.

I learned in that moment the lesson that Qohelet is trying to teach us in this passage: there is a time for everything, and this was not the *appropriate* time for Patchy's retirement. Therefore, I went back out to the burn barrel, picked him up, and brought him back inside.

Heidi eventually came to realize that Patchy's white trail was only getting worse and would not improve. That being so, she began to spend more time with Super Bear. Then one day she volunteered on her own, "It's time for Patchy to go," and he departed. That was the appropriate time for his retirement.

3. God's Order Is Significant and Necessary

God's order is significant because it provides the framework for all of creation. It establishes the laws of nature, the regularity of patterns in life, and the characters within creation. God has placed humanity within this framework. God's order does not void our free will, but it does limit our possibilities and knowledge.

God's order is necessary because it provides the basis for divine-human interaction. According to Ecclesiastes 3:14, the purpose of God's order is "so that people will fear him." Fear, here, does not refer to a frightened, emotional reaction to being in the presence of almighty God. It is to revere God, to reverence him, to respect him, and to worship him. It implies submitting to his lordship and obediently following his directions for our lives. It opens the door for divine-human conversation. Electricity keeps our homes warm in the winter, cool in the summer, and illuminated in the darkness. We need not be afraid of electricity, but we do well to respect its power to destroy if we take it lightly or foolishly.

The concept of fearing God lies at the heart of the wisdom theology (Job 1:1; 28:28; Ps. 33:8; Prov. 1:7; Eccles. 12:13) because it is the wisest action we can take in life. We will be out of sorts with God's order until we can say with the psalmist, "My times are in your hands" (Ps. 31:15 [16 HB]). Our lives run best when we are following God's order and timing. Humans are the only creatures who can recognize this and respond to it.

4. God's Order Cannot Be Fully Comprehended by Human Beings

Scholars have struggled with the meaning of the word "eternity" ('ōlām) in Ecclesiastes 3:11b: "He has also set eternity in the human heart; yet no one can fathom what God has done from beginning to end." We need not get into the scholarly debate about the word's meaning here. Here, Qohelet was not referring to the human desire for the kind of eternal life God alone enjoys. In this OT setting, it most likely refers to a desire to understand the nature and purpose of God's activities *within time* "from beginning to end."

What is the big picture God has in mind for planet earth and human society? If we knew that, we would understand the ultimate meaning of life. Unfortunately, according to Qohelet, we will never know that. There are reasons for God's actions and times, but human beings are not privy to them. We know there is order in the world and that God is the author of that order. At times, we are aware of what that order looks like as it unfolds. We also may come to believe that all of God's actions are appropriate when they occur. That is as far as we can go in our reasoning. We will not know any more unless God chooses to reveal more about himself and his activities.

By nature, God keeps his overall plan for the world to himself. No one knows why he does certain things at certain times, and it is useless to ask. The times he has chosen for the fourteen pairs of opposites in 3:1-8 remain a mystery. That being the case, it is impossible to know "what is truly going on in the world" (Towner 1997, 306). Thus the ultimate meaning of life will always be unknown, as Qohelet sees it.

5. God's Order Provides for Enjoyment in Life

The fact that humans are not privy to knowledge about ultimate meanings and future events frustrated Qohelet. He felt that he was living his life in the dark. This prompted his favorite word—"vanity." Still, it did not discourage him from living a happy and satisfied life in his day-to-day activities.

Here is where Qohelet has a profound and positive word of advice for people in the twenty-first century (Eccles. 3:12-13): "I know that there is nothing better for people than to be happy and to do good while they live. That each of them may eat and drink, and find satisfaction in all their toil—this is the gift of God." What does this mean?

First, we may not know the future (v. 11), and we may not be able to change the times that God has chosen (v. 14), but we can still enjoy our lives by focusing on the simple things that God has provided (→ the earlier sermon "The Search for Meaning in Life," p. 41). Qohelet calls these simple things gifts from God (v. 13). Our food, our family, our friends, and our work are some of God's ways of blessing us and giving us a good life from beginning to end. If we will focus our attention and energies on these simple things and not chafe against the overall order that God has established for our universe, we can create for ourselves a life of joy.

We will probably never arrive at an understanding of the ultimate meaning of life, and we will probably never comprehend all the complexities of life with its good and its bad times. However, we can enjoy our time on earth as a gift from the one who created us. These words fly in the face of materialism and greed, and they counter typical human egotism. Qohelet's word to us is that real happiness is not found in self-centered activities or in the pursuit of material things. It is found in accepting and enjoying the simple things of life that God provides. By focusing on these basic human needs, we can rise above our troubles and find satisfaction and meaning even in the worst of times.

Second, it means that happiness and satisfaction are a part of God's desire for every human being. God does not want us living lives of confusion, anger, and depression. He wants us to experience good emotional well-being. If we fear him (v. 14) and live according to the order he has embedded in our universe, we can truly enjoy our lives amid both the good and the bad around us. We can choose to accept whatever comes our way in life with a good attitude. "The crucial question is not what happens, but how we handle it" (Davidson 1986, 24).

Third, the passage means that we should align our attitude toward our work/toil with God's perspective (→ the next sermon, "The Meaning of Work," p. 65). Qohelet mentions that one of the avenues for finding satisfaction and meaning in life is through our work. In addition to providing income to put food on our table and clothes on our back, it provides order and purpose to our lives as we work alongside others toward a common goal. Our work becomes even more important when we put it in a Christian context of service to God. We are benefiting not only our employer and ourselves but also God's kingdom.

6. God's Order Is Permanent and Complete

This passage moves to its conclusion with a word about God's sovereignty. His actions in the world are permanent and complete (Eccles. 1:15; 3:14; 7:13). They cannot be changed by humanity. There is no need to improve them because they are perfect and right in God's mind. Each event fits exactly where it belongs.

Qohelet viewed this as something negative. It made him frustrated that he could not change things in the world that he thought needed improvement. It also troubled him that God kept the reasons for his plans hidden from humanity. Job had a similar negative impression of God (Job 9:22-24; 21:17-26; 24:7-17, 25). Both Qohelet and Job were frustrated that God refused to share his plans with them.

However, there is a more positive way to react to the problem raised in Ecclesiastes 3:14. First, it is important and beneficial to us that there is order in the world rather than chaos. Just as in any sports event, there are rules to the game of life. We may not understand God's structure of the world, and we may have questions about the timing of certain events. However, it should be very reassuring to us that God has placed us in an ordered world—a world created by and still governed by God, who has a plan. We should be grateful that God knows what he is doing, because our world does not always make sense to us. Too many times, evil and chaos seem to have the upper hand. As those who are following God's plan know, he is the one who is really in control.

Second, our lives run best when we adjust them to God's order. We may not want to do so, because we sometimes think our plans are right and God's are wrong. However, God knows best. Job learned this important lesson when God took him on a tour of creation (Job 38–41). According to all the sages, the wise person has learned to fear God and follow his leading (Eccles. 3:14; 8:12-13; 12:13; Job 28:28; 42:1-6; Prov. 1:7; 15:33). Acceptance of God's authority means living a humble life, reverencing God because of who he is, and thanking him for the simple things he has provided. By doing so, we prove our acceptance of his plans and order for our world.

Qohelet had much the same reaction to God's actions in the world as Job. Both were critical of God's ways (Job 9:22-24; 21:17-26; 24:1-17, 25; Eccles. 1:2, 12-15; 8:16-17). Both believed that God did not treat humanity properly. Qohelet called these actions vanity, whereas Job called them injustice.

Job eventually changed his mind about God (Job 42:1-6). Why did Qohelet not? Why did Qohelet continue to maintain his skepticism of God throughout the entire book? The answer probably lies in the fact that Job received a visit from God whereas Qohelet did not. God's self-revelation caused Job to reevaluate his understanding of God and of himself. Qohelet apparently never had the opportunity to hear directly from God. We can only wonder whether he would have acknowledged his ignorance and submitted his life to God if he had had a similar divine visitation.

This side of the coming of Christ–Immanuel, "God with us," can we claim we have not been granted the supreme divine visitation? Are the life and teachings of Jesus not enough? Must God give you a personal visitation? If he did, would you abandon your skepticism and criticism and offer your life to be used for his glory? Why not ask him to meet you right now? He is probably just waiting for you to ask.

Possible Sermon Titles: "The Pendulum of Time," "The Value of the Simple Things," "God's Gift of Enjoyment," "A Suitable Time for Everything," "A Time to Tear Down and a Time to Build," "What Goes Around Comes Around," "A Time for This and That," "In God's Time"

V. THE VALUE OF WORK AND THE IMPORTANCE OF WORKING TOGETHER (ECCLES. 4:1-16)

The Meaning of Work (Eccles. 4:4-12)

Work is a daily part of most people's lives, yet few sermons ever address this topic. Ecclesiastes mentions the topic several times, and these can be supplemented with a few NT passages. The following sermon idea draws on all these passages. It would be an appropriate sermon for the Sunday before Labor Day.

We have already seen that work is one of the few things that can add meaning to human existence (→ the earlier sermons "The Search for Meaning in Life," p. 41, and "In His Time," p. 51). According to Qohelet, work was one of the simple things, along with food and drink, which can make our lives enjoyable here and now (Eccles. 2:24; 3:13, 22). Thus Qohelet urged his readers to engage in meaningful work. Work provides a daily rhythm to life that helps organize our time (3:1-8). In addition, it supplies the means to purchase our family's food, clothing, and shelter. Let's look at some of the points Qohelet makes about work.

1. Work Is the Lot of Humankind

Qohelet strongly believed that work is an assignment that God has given every human being. He called it our "lot" or "portion" in life (Eccles. 3:22; 5:18-19 [17-18 HB]; 9:9). This thought draws from Genesis 3:17-19, 23: God's curse on Adam's disobedience. Adam and all his descendants would have to work in order to eat. Their food would no longer be supplied directly by God. They would have to toil for it, battling thorns and thistles and sweating profusely.

Not all people willingly accept God's assignment. They do not like work. They are lazy and seek every possible means of avoiding their lot in life. This attitude probably developed in their formative years, playing hooky and failing to turn in homework.

Qohelet called such people fools (Eccles. 4:5). He warned that their avoidance of work would lead them to failure. The literal translation of 4:5b is fools "consume their own flesh" (NRSV). That is, refusal to work would lead to a lack of food, which would force them to eat their own flesh. Metaphorically, the final consequence of foolish behavior is self-destruction. Proverbs echoes this conviction (1:32; 6:10-11; 10:8, 10, 14; 14:1; 16:22; 24:33-34). Proverbs also makes it clear that the avoidance of work is a moral issue; it is a sign of the rejection of God (10:23; 13:19; 14:9; also Ps. 14:1).

The NT also warns against idleness/laziness. Paul warned the Thessalonians "to keep away from every believer who is idle and disruptive and does not live according to the teaching you received from us" (2 Thess. 3:6). His guidance to them was, "The one who is unwilling to work shall not eat" (v. 10). Lazy Christians would turn into leeches and lose respect from the people in their community (1 Thess. 4:12).

For some overly competitive people, work is a regular activity, but only because it enables them to get ahead of others. This competitiveness is driven by envy and rivalry (Eccles. 4:4). Qohelet's claim that *all* work is the result of envy is hyperbolic—deliberate exaggeration for literary effect.

In fact, much work is due to talent, creativity, and a desire to provide for one's family. There is no question that envy and rivalry do rear their ugly heads in the business world, driving some to attempt to better their competitors at all costs. Such an attitude will never satisfy; it will likely lead to a loss of health, both physical and emotional (Prov. 14:30). Qohelet claimed such work behavior was simply "chasing after the wind" (Eccles. 4:4). No one can ever achieve superiority over everyone else. On the ladder of life, there is always someone who is one rung ahead of us and someone just behind us nipping at our heals.

Qohelet recommended the golden mean—the middle ground between avoiding work altogether and letting work become our master.

Ecclesiastes 4:6 speaks of the difference between two hands grasping for too much work and one hand accomplishing what it is fully capable of achieving. The former leads to stress, discontent, and a sense of meaninglessness. The latter leads to tranquility (see 5:12; Prov. 15:16-17; 16:8; 17:1). "If the choice is between less gained in repose and quiet and twice that amount gained in toil-full strife, choose less" (Duncan 2017, 61).

This is illustrated in Qohelet's example of the lonely workaholics who suddenly came to their senses and realized that all their dogged efforts had been in vain (Eccles. 4:7-8). They wasted their best years in self-centered activities that brought them nothing but unhappiness. Qohelet was not criticizing healthy achievement. He merely pointed out the meaninglessness of making work our god or master.

2. Work Is a Gift from God

Many people never imagine that God is responsible for helping them find meaningful work. They attribute their jobs to other factors, including their own efforts in making good grades in school, their extraordinary ability to sell themselves to a future employer, knowing the right people, and being in the right place at the right time.

It is true that sometimes these factors enter into our employment. But such a view may be self-centered or focused on dumb luck. Qohelet believed that God played a substantial role in helping people secure good jobs and in enjoying them. Such jobs come "from the hand of God" (Eccles. 2:24). They are the "gift of God" (3:13; 5:19 [18 HB]). Therefore, we should not "disparage work" but regard it as our "ethical duty" (Brown 2011, 129).

If our jobs are due to God's guidance and intervention, then we should do them well. Qohelet urged his readers, "Do [them] with all your might" (9:10). Similarly, Paul encouraged his readers to work at their jobs "with all your heart" and to consider their jobs as "working for the Lord" (Col. 3:23; see Col. 3:23-24; Eph. 6:5-8). Those who regard their secular work as an opportunity to serve Christ will certainly have a different attitude toward their work than those who see themselves as just working for a company or a boss.

3. God Intended for Work to Be Enjoyed

There are different human reactions to work. Some see it as just repetitive, toilsome labor (→ the earlier sermon "Vanity of Vanities,"

p. 33). Their job puts food on the table, but just barely. They know that no matter how hard they work, they will never get all of their bills paid. So why should they exert themselves?

Other workers *like* the industry they are in but do not like their particular job. They think they are overworked, underpaid, and underappreciated by their boss—they have little chance for advancement. They consider their job a rat race, a grind, or a dead end, and they eagerly look forward to retirement.

Because Qohelet was aware of this all-too-common feeling, he used the terms "toil" (*ʿāmāl*) and "toilsome labor" twenty-one times as synonyms for work (e.g., Eccles. 1:3; 2:10-11, 18-19; 3:9, 13; 4:4, 8). The Hebrew word means "arduous, wearisome labor" (Fox 2004, xviii). He wanted his readers to know he empathized with their feelings.

Some other people work mainly to fill their lives with good things (6:7). There is nothing wrong with wanting to improve one's economic status. The problem with this perspective is that human desires for material things can never be satisfied. The more they get, the more they want (5:10 [9 HB]; 6:9; Prov. 16:26). The more they want, the more work they take on.

Those who work simply to acquire more have a deep gnawing inside that leads to stress and dissatisfaction. Those who work merely for material gain eventually learn that all the possessions they acquire will disappear when they die, if not sooner through misfortune (Eccles. 2:17-23; 5:13-16 [12-15 HB]; 6:1-2). Jesus's parable of the rich fool made this same point (Luke 12:15-21). "Life does not consist in an abundance of possessions" (v. 15).

None of the three attitudes to work outlined above are the way God intended for people to live. Qohelet was convinced that God wanted people to enjoy their work (Eccles. 2:24; 3:12-13, 22; 8:15). They should have great satisfaction in going to work each day. They should work, not for selfish gain or to get ahead of someone else, but for the enjoyment of using their talents and skills for the glory of God and for others. Paul echoed this thought in 1 Corinthians 10:31. Qohelet advised his readers, "Be content with your job and earnings and live in the moment, for the future is not guaranteed" (Eccles. 9:10-12, author's paraphrase).

4. Work Is Best Carried Out in Community

In Ecclesiastes 4:7-12, Qohelet contrasted people who saw their work as a lonely, single endeavor with those who experienced the benefits of working in community. The person in verses 7-8 was single. He had no family, no fellowship, no one with whom to share his experiences. As a result, he focused his attention on his work and became a workaholic. Night and day, he forced himself to grow his business. His wealth kept growing, but he was never satisfied. He continued to seek more.

However, one day he suddenly realized that his life had no enjoyment. His Scrooge-like attitude of "all work and no play" was a dead end, because he had no one with whom to share his wealth or to leave it to after his death. So why was he working himself to death? He thought of all the joy he had missed over the years. Obsession with this work was costing him dearly.

The first-person quotation in verse 8 characterizes what he said to himself when the truth finally dawned on him. Some interpreters think this may also be Qohelet's confession, as he identified with this lonely man. Qohelet did not say whether this realization caused the man to change his life. His only comment was that this life situation is meaningless and miserable (v. 8). Wealth achieved through constant rivalry and striving brings no satisfaction.

In contrast, the person who has a partner/companion in life has many advantages over the single person. Many commentators have applied this passage to marriage, and rightfully so. However, it can equally apply to parent-child relationships, sibling connections, business partnerships, and good friendships.

Qohelet mentioned four benefits two people have over one. First, more can be accomplished (v. 9). Two people can get much more done than one. Second, in times of failure and crisis, one can pull the other one up (v. 10). Should failure occur, the recovery time is significantly less when one has a companion. Safety experts today apply this same principle to would-be deep-sea diving, hiking, mountain climbing, cross-country skiing, and hunting. Third, the heat of one person warms another (v. 11). This could apply literally in a lost outdoor excursion or an unheated home in the winter. It also applies to the emotional and relational warmth others provide through their presence and encouragement. Fourth, when attacked, whether physically or verbally, two people have a greater chance of defending themselves than one (v. 12). Those who survived the challenges of the Oregon Trail learned that circling the wagons better prepared them to fend off attacks. One wagon could not provide protection from every side.

The intended lesson of Qohelet's teaching is that life as a loner is "a miserable business" (v. 8). He could not support rugged individualism; companionship has many more benefits.

Ecclesiastes 4:7-12 clearly shows the importance of community. It is true not only of work environments but also of most other life activities. In the early 1970s, Reuben Welch wisely explored this timeless truth: *We Really Do Need Each Other* (1973). If two together are better than one, how much more effective is a friendship of three (v. 12)?

Qohelet illuminated many of the destructive attitudes many have about their work. It was not good in Qohelet's day, and it is still not good today. Many have negative views of their jobs. They do not like the position they are in; they are looking for another job or just holding on until their age and finances allow them an early retirement. Perhaps you are in that situation. If so, maybe Qohelet's insights can help you gain a different perspective.

If we see our job as a gift from God, it will make us more positive in our attitude toward our work. If we believe God wants us to enjoy our work, we will look for ways to make that happen. We will be less inclined to envy others and less interested in becoming a workaholic. If we recognize the importance of community, we will attempt to gain more friends at work and show an interest in their personal lives.

Brown adds one further thought. If we realize that our work does not define us, we can rest assured that *God* knows who we are. That is what really matters.

Human identity does not rest on achievements. A person is more than the sum of his or her successes and failures. The message of Scripture is that one need not be enslaved or alienated by the toil of work, for human identity and destiny rest on what God does and has done, rather than on what human beings strive to achieve. Created in the image of God, humankind *shares* in God's own creative activity, both in work and in rest. Rather than absorbed in their own achievements, human beings find their true vocation in discipleship. (Brown 2011, 131-32)

Possible Sermon Titles: "Work or Toil?" "Why Go to Work Every Day?" "Do You Enjoy Your Job?" "Are You Wishing Your Life Away? "You Know You Can't Take It with You, Right?"

VI. DEATH AWAITS US ALL (ECCLES. 9:1-18)

Waiting for God (Eccles. 9:1-12)

From 1990 to 1994, the BBC produced a sitcom series called *Waiting for God*. Each episode focused on the humorous adventures of a group of elderly people at a retirement home in England. The main characters were all within a few years of death, but that did not stop them from mischievously creating problems for the staff and among themselves. One of the themes was that people can enjoy life at any age. Young people do not have a corner on fun.

Americans live in a culture that rarely talks about death. The subject makes us uncomfortable. We live at a fast pace, acting as if death will never walk down our street and knock on our door. Even the death of over a million Americans from the COVID-19 pandemic did not increase the conversation about the topic. On more than one occasion, I have conducted funerals for people who have left their families fully unprepared for their passing because no one dared to talk about this subject. Those who were left behind had no idea of what to put in a memorial service; where to find a will, bank accounts, life insurance policies, deeds, and even keys; and what to do with the house, car, and possessions. A few written instructions or even a one-hour conversation before death would have helped these families immensely.

In contrast to contemporary American culture, the subject of death is a prominent topic in Ecclesiastes. The author mentions it in more than a dozen passages (Eccles. 2:14-16; 3:2, 19-21; 4:2-3; 5:15-16 [14-15 HB]; 6:3-6; 7:1-2, 4, 17, 26; 8:8; 9:2-12; 11:8; 12:5-7). We would do well to spend some time on this topic if we want to understand Qohelet's thinking. Here are his main points.

1. Death Is a Certainty for Everyone

We all will die (Eccles. 9:2). No matter what our status in life is, no matter what our family heritage is, no matter what possessions and achievements we may have accumulated, no matter whether we have lived a righteous life or a wicked one, we will die. It is certain. Even the sages with all their wisdom would die just like everyone else (2:15-16).

Over the centuries, people have looked for a fountain of youth—a place where people could go to drink the water or bathe in a pool to lengthen their life. Written records of such a place go back to the time of the Greek historian Herodotus (fifth century BC). In the New World of the Americas, the Spanish explorer Ponce de León is most famously associated with searching for such a fountain in Florida. It is said that native people in the Caribbean told him that such a place existed. There is an archaeological park in Saint Augustine, Florida, that claims to be the place where Ponce de León set foot in AD 1513. However, the story is more mythological than historical. Ponce de León never mentioned searching for a fountain of youth in his writings. Moreover, no one has ever discovered a genuine fountain of youth.

In more recent times, scientists have focused their attention on finding a drug that would lengthen life. Again, no miracle drug affecting everyone's length of life has been discovered. It is true that new drugs have helped to cure many diseases that used to take people's lives at an early age. It is also true that the average human lifespan has lengthened considerably in the last century due to better nutrition, more exercise, and a better understanding of the human body. Thus many more people are living into their eighties and nineties, and some even to one hundred. That was a rarity a century ago. Still, death cannot be avoided. Millions have died before us, and millions more will follow.

2. The Time of Our Death Is Unknown

According to Qohelet, there is "a time to be born and a time to die" (Eccles. 3:2), and "no one knows when their hour will come" (9:12; see 8:8). Some people die without any warning at all. A heart attack or a car accident suddenly takes them away. Others get very close to death's door, and then they rally and live for many more years. Of course, we all would like to know the future. If we did, we could make money in the stock market. We could put off buying life insurance until the day before we die. We could become millionaires by placing a big bet on the winner of a major sports competition. But the future is unknown. Perhaps that is for the best because we might see some really nasty things that are coming to meet us in the days ahead.

3. We Will Lose All Our Possessions and Achievements When We Die

Most people work very hard to get ahead in life. Over time, they gradually build up status at their workplace, influence with other people, and some measure of wealth—perhaps a house on a piece of land, a car, and so forth. According to Qohelet, we can take none of these things with us after death. We come naked into this world, and we leave in the same condition (Eccles. 5:15-16 [14-15 HB]). Job came to the same conclusion (Job 1:20-21). Further, the memory of our lives will be forgotten completely after we die. Even our names will disappear into oblivion (Eccles. 9:5-6). This was terribly frustrating to Qohelet. Why even bother to work if it gains you no benefit in the long run (1:3)?

4. We Have No Hope for Anything Better after Death

Qohelet's understanding of the afterlife was no different from that of other Israelites of the OT era. The place that people go after death was called Sheol. It was a dark, quiet place located under the ground. It was filled with the shades/ghosts of the deceased. Their bodies returned to dust (Eccles. 3:20). Everyone went to Sheol—both the righteous and sinners. Even the animals went there according to Qohelet (vv. 19-20). There was nothing to look forward to in Sheol. God was not there, and no rewards for a good life were given. Life after death was just a meaningless existence with no hope for anything better.

Beyond that Qohelet leaves us confused, for his words are contradictory. In 4:1-3 and 6:3-6, he mentioned that the dead are happier than the living because they do not have to see or experience all the bad things in the world. Their life's journey is over, and so is their contact with human trouble and evil. Even better yet is a person who has never been born or is stillborn. Such persons are extremely fortunate because they have never had to face trouble. Job's sentiments were much the same (Job 3:11-19). Qohelet continued this thought with different imagery in Ecclesiastes 7:1-2, 4. There he pointed out that "the day of death [was] better than the day of birth" (v. 1), and "it is better to go to a house of mourning than to go to a house of feasting" (v. 2).

However, in 9:4-6 Qohelet praised the living over the dead. The problem with the dead is that their names and activities are soon forgotten, and no rewards are given in Sheol. At least the living know that life can be enjoyed and may get better. God may even honor them with a reward before they die. Thus "even a live dog is better off than a dead lion!" (v. 4).

Perhaps 9:4-6 can be reconciled with the verses in Ecclesiastes 4, 6, and 7. Note that Ecclesiastes 9 referred to the finality of death, not to experiences after death. Nothing can be changed after death, so there is no hope for the dead.

5. Life Is Senseless

Qohelet's entire life was devoted to trying to find the ultimate meaning of life. His experiments recounted in Ecclesiastes 1:12–2:26 were focused on this goal (→ the earlier sermon "The Search for Meaning in Life," p. 41). In the end, he knew he had failed. Life remains a mystery because God has not instructed human beings about its meaning.

For Qohelet, not even the sages with all their emphasis on right living and making wise decisions understood the real meaning of life. Qohelet was a member of the group of people called sages. Their philosophy of life had been around for hundreds of years. We find evidence of this in writings from Mesopotamia and Egypt that go back to 2700 BC. The book of Proverbs largely reflects the optimistic view of the sages of the ancient world. These people believed that God honors those who are righteous, honest, and faithful to him and that he rewards them with long life, wealth, success, and happiness (Prov. 3:1-18).

However, Qohelet could not accept this view of life. For him, life remained a mystery—confusing and uncertain. God had not shared the key that unlocks this mystery, and even the wise were left in the dark about its meaning. Life is like a big, new LEGO set a kid gets for

Christmas arriving in one giant Ziploc bag. Sadly, it is without an instruction booklet or a picture of the finished product. There is no way to know if all of the pieces were included or if there might be some extras. We could probably attempt to create something out of the pieces we have, but it would not be exactly like the manufacturer's intention. Our efforts to put every piece in its proper place would be futile.

Similarly, our efforts to understand life and make good decisions are doomed to failure because we are unaware of life's ultimate meaning. In fact, we do not even know if God will react with love or hatred toward us, because he treats everyone the same (Eccles. 9:1-2).

What was even more grievous for Qohelet was the thought that humans were no better off regarding death than animals (3:18-20). They also die. Birds, fish, insects, and plants–every living thing eventually dies. The only difference between humans and animals, as Qohelet saw it, was that God had placed the knowledge of eternity in the minds of humans (v. 11). But this only makes us more miserable, because we know that God is eternal and all-knowing and we are not. Why has God not rewarded the wise and the righteous with a more adequate understanding of life, more like what he enjoys? Qohelet had no answer to this question

In Ecclesiastes 9:11-12, Qohelet shared a fundamental principle that drove his belief in the senselessness of life. Most people think the fastest runner always wins a race and the strongest army always wins a battle. Likewise, most think that wisdom, intelligence, and education are sure pathways to adequate food, wealth, and popularity. People who make wise choices and have talents and skills should be rewarded with good, successful lives.

As shown in Aesop's fable of the Tortoise and the Hare, popular expectations are not always correct. Rewards are not inevitable. "Time and chance" are always lurking behind the scenes ready to trip people up. Misfortune, accidents, disease, natural disasters, evil people, and even death may show up unexpectedly at any time and totally disrupt the expected outcome that seems so obvious at first glance.

Qohelet certainly knew the view of other sages that wisdom and righteousness always lead to divine blessing and success (Prov. 2:1-22; 3:1-18). Apparently, he had observed too many exceptions to the rule—situations in life that did not work out as expected. Too many good people had experienced hard times and met an early death, and too many bad people had enjoyed success. We do not know if Qohelet was aware of the book of Job. If he had been, he probably would have pointed to Job as proof of his views. Job was the most righteous person of his generation, but he also suffered the most horrendous losses of his generation, and it was all approved by God.

Life just never seems to work out as planned or expected. We can never be sure of what will happen to us because the events in life are beyond our control. This thought drove Qohelet crazy. However, he could do nothing about it, except observe it and call it senseless. Vanity!

6. What Should People Do If the Meaning of Life Is a Mystery?

If Qohelet was right—that life is a mystery, what should be our reaction? Qohelet's answer to this question was that people could experience joy in their lives if they avoid worrying about the future and trying to get ahead of others. Instead of worrying, people should make good use of the time they have been given on earth. They should engage in life's activities with all their might because such activities will end when they die (Eccles. 9:10). If people accept what they have and use it wisely in the time they have, their intrinsic reward will be self-satisfaction. They will find that their food and drink, their work, and their marriage and other relationships will provide them with "gladness" and "a joyful heart" (9:7; see vv. 7-9; 2:24-25). Therefore, Qohelet urged his readers, "Seek to enjoy the normal activities of life, for God wants you to enjoy them" (9:7, author's paraphrase).

We should note that Qohelet did not encourage people to trust in God in the same sense as Jesus taught in the Sermon on the Mount (Matt. 6:25-34). Qohelet's emphasis was on the importance of right human attitudes and activities that could bring joy. Jesus focused more on asking God to forgive our sins, turning our lives over to God, and trusting him to take care of our needs.

The writers of the NT somewhat followed Qohelet's lead. They all supported the first three of Qohelet's findings.

First, we all will die a physical death because of our relationship to Adam (1 Cor. 15:22; Heb. 9:27). Jesus noted that death was not reserved for only the worst of sinners (Luke 13:1-5). It happens to everyone.

Second, none of us knows the date of our death. In fact, says James, we "do not even know what will happen tomorrow" (James 4:14). The future, including the day of our death, is unknown to all of us. Those who claim differently are ignorant and arrogant (vv. 15-16).

Third, our possessions in this life remain in this world. None of them go with us into the next life. In the parable of the rich fool, Jesus talked about a rich man who had much wealth and was enjoying an easy life (Luke 12:16-21). When he died that night, all of his possessions went to others. The same was the case in Jesus's parable of the rich man and Lazarus (16:19-31). Upon death, Lazarus ended up with Abraham, while the rich man went to Hades. There he lost all of his wealth and luxurious attire. He was in great agony and did not even have water to drink.

However, NT writers had a significantly different view on Qohelet's points no. 4 and no. 5. This was partly due to changes within Judaism. Under the influence of the Pharisees, many Jews in Jesus's day had accepted a belief in (1) the resurrection of the dead at the time of the Messiah's coming and (2) a final judgment of all human beings. They also believed that there are two separate destinations in the afterlife—a place for the righteous (heaven) and a place for the wicked (hell). Christians, following Jesus's teachings, accepted these beliefs.

Most decisive for Christians was their understanding of Jesus's own death and resurrection. Paul pointed out the significance of this in 1 Corinthians 15. There he spoke of Jesus's resurrection as the lynchpin for Christian theology. Without Christ's resurrection, there would be no Christian faith (v. 14). Without Christ's resurrection, there would be no salvation from sin (v. 17). Without Christ's resurrection, there would be no resurrection of human beings (vv. 12-18). There would be no new life (v. 22), no final triumph over evil powers (vv. 24-25), no victory over death (vv. 26, 54-55), and no transformation of our mortal bodies into spiritual bodies (vv. 42-49). The resurrection was crucially significant in Paul's thinking. He knew the meaning and importance of Jesus's statement in John 11:25 (NRSV): "I am the resurrection and the life. Those who believe in me, even though they die, will live, and everyone who lives and believes in me will never die."

Because of Christ's death and resurrection, his followers are no longer plagued with Qohelet's sad, pessimistic view of human existence. Christian life *does make sense*—both now and after death. In this life, we have salvation from sin and the presence of God's Holy Spirit to teach and encourage us (3:16; 14:15-27). In the next life, we have the promise of a blessed eternity with God (14:1-4). So whose philosophy of life makes better sense to you—Qohelet's or Jesus's?

Folks, death is coming whether we plan for it or not. We can thank Qohelet for reminding us that death is a reality for all of us. For some, it may be just around the corner. We had better get prepared.

Possible Sermon Titles: "Death—the Great Leveler," "Time and Chance," "*Carpe Diem* (Seize the Day)," "The Fountain of Youth: A Reality or a Pipe Dream?" "Are You Ready for the Next Life?" "Death Is Coming, Like It or Not"

VII. REMEMBER YOUR CREATOR (ECCLES. 11:7–12:8)

Youth and Old Age (11:7–12:8)

This passage is clearly divided into two sections with a connecting verse in the middle. The first section (11:7-10) is an exhortation to young people to enjoy the present. The second (12:1-8) is a dark description of senior adulthood, which Qohelet fashions into a warning about the future.

Qohelet offered no precise age indicators, but he was probably addressing teenaged young people. We must keep in mind that people in the ancient world lived about half as long on average as people do today. By the end of their teen years, most people had already lived about half of their lifetime. Thus education needed to start early, and it needed to cover the essentials quickly.

Today, we think of youth as an intermediate stage between childhood and adulthood. It is an important preparation period for the societal requirements placed on adults. Youth need these years to learn (1) various useful skills, such as occupational skills, social skills, financial skills, and emotional skills; (2) important bodies of knowledge, such as characteristics of the natural world and the history of humanity in prior eras; and (3) habits of discipline for their minds and bodies. Youth also need education in how to respond to the dangers of life—bad people, bad activities, and bad ideas. We could add further descriptions of the teen years based on modern studies of child development. The point is that young people are at a critical stage in the development of human beings. Every teen needs significant input from parents, schools, and the church during this time.

1. Enjoy Life While You Can (Eccles. 11:7-10)

In Ecclesiastes 11:7-10, Qohelet gave four words of advice to students in his classroom.

First, enjoy your youthful years (vv. 8-9). Be happy while you can. Seize the day of opportunity. Make the most of your time *now* when you have the energy and strength to do the things you want to do. "Far from moping around in despair, [Qohelet] would have us really live while we are alive" (Towner 1997, 356). The reason is that dark days are coming when you will not be happy, when you will not have energy, and when life may overwhelm you with its problems. Further, the older you get, the closer you are to death.

Second, follow your heart (v. 9). Be curious about life. Ask good questions. Go where your eyes lead you. In your teen years, you are not burdened with job and family responsibilities. You are free to investigate life and try new things. Qohelet's recommendations would probably include traveling abroad, visiting other countries, and trying new foods.

At the same time, Qohelet offered a word of caution. Remember that God will hold you accountable for all your activities, so do not go overboard in trying to live a carefree life. Do not ruin the rest of your life by making foolish decisions while you are young.

Qohelet's second point might not seem to be shared by other biblical authors. Other passages in the OT offer a necessary counterpoint. For example, in Numbers 15:39, God exhorted Israel not to pursue the lusts of their "hearts and eyes." Proverbs often warned young people to avoid the corrupting influence of bad companions (Prov. 1:10-19), loose women (5:1-23; 6:20-35; 7:1-27), and Lady Foolishness (9:13-18). Even youths should obey the covenant (Numbers) and avoid temptations that would lead them away from God (Proverbs). Qohelet's emphasis is completely different.

Third, do not be anxious about tomorrow (Eccles. 11:10). Yes, there are legitimate concerns in life that need our attention and should be addressed. But anxiety is a step beyond legitimate concerns. It manifests itself in continual, debilitating worrying. It robs people of their joy and may lead them to severe depression (Prov. 12:25). Many issues we worry about are beyond our control. Anxiety will not solve them anyway.

In the Sermon on the Mount, Jesus urged his followers to avoid anxiety about the future (Matt. 6:25-34). He said that God would take care of his followers just as he watches over the birds of the air and the flowers in the fields. Instead of worrying about tomorrow, people of faith should seek to follow God's guidance and live righteously today. Jesus promised that such persons would have all their needs met. Likewise, Peter and Paul urged believers to present their anxieties to God rather than bottle them up inside (1 Pet. 5:7; Phil. 4:6-7). God will give peace to those who put their trust in him.

Fourth, cast off your bodily aches and pains (Eccles. 11:10). Qohelet was not exactly clear about what he meant by "the troubles of your body" (v. 10). Young people do not normally have the typical pains that plague the aged. Perhaps he encouraged avoiding activities that could lead to broken bones, wounds, and concussions. The destructive effects of drugs and alcohol on one's body could also have been in his mind. In any case, Qohelet urged people to remove anything that might cause them physical pain and would hinder their enjoyment of life. Life is too short to have it ruined by physical distress.

Of course, some people have no choice in that. They were born with physical deformities and inherited diseases. Qohelet's advice was to not aggravate our physical condition by engaging in destructive and/or senseless activities.

Because both mind and body are mentioned in verse 10, clearly Qohelet was "affirming a holistic approach to enjoyment: one should keep both mind and body free of unnecessary discomfort" (Duncan 2017, 169). He urged the young to make the most of their youthful years. If young people followed Qohelet's advice, their lives would be "sweet" like the warming, nourishing, energizing light of the sun (v. 7).

2. Old Age and Death Are Coming (Eccles. 12:1b-8)

As we move into Ecclesiastes 12, we are confronted with one of the darkest sections in Ecclesiastes. Towner suggests that to achieve the greatest oral effect, preachers should read verses 1-7 using a descending pitch in their voice and a slower and slower pace, like a clock running down. "The poem is a great inclined plane dropping to the lowest range of the voice and the lowest decibel of sound and culminating in extinction!" (1997, 356). Verse 8 should then be read in full volume to put a final exclamation point on the overarching theme of the book—VANITY! (NRSV).

The content of the passage is straightforward. It is a poetic description of the final years of life, culminating in death and a funeral procession. The numerous figurative images have inspired a range of interpretations among both Christian and Jewish commentators. Some have tried to relate them allegorically to parts of the body that begin to decline in old age.

For example, the dimming of the sun, moon, and stars (v. 2) is associated with the loss of light as one's eyesight fails—probably due to cataracts. The trembling of "the keepers of the house" (v. 3) seems to be related to the weakening of the extremities and the onset of nervous shaking. The cessation of work by "grinders" (v. 3) is linked to the loss of teeth.

However, some of the proposed associations are fanciful and arbitrary. It is impossible to make a direct connection between all the images in this passage and parts of the body, so this interpretation has problems.

Other scholars have sought an eschatological interpretation that ties the images to a future military conflict or even the end of the world. We know that some of the OT prophets used imagery about the darkening of the sun, moon, and stars and general terror in the land in their descriptions of the day of the Lord (Isa. 2:12-21; 13:6-13; Jer. 46:10; Ezek. 32:1-16; Joel 2:1-11; 3:14-16; Amos 5:18, 20; Zeph. 1:14-18; Zech. 14:1-7). As with the previous interpretations, not all the images in this section of Ecclesiastes can be connected with end-time events.

The simplest and best interpretation is the literal one. Yes, there are a number of figurative images, but they are not allegorical or eschatological. They are simply poetic ways of describing the final years of human life. Old age is like a gloomy storm that darkens the sky and blots out the celestial bodies that provide light (Eccles. 12:2). A second metaphor compares aging to a great estate that was once busy with activity but falls into decay and quietness (vv. 3-4). Its managers and servants are fearful that they will no longer be needed when the estate owner dies. A third metaphor personifies aging as an old, white-haired man who shuffles around slowly like a dying grasshopper. He is afraid to go outside because of a fear of falling (v. 5a). The fourth image is that of a funeral procession. Wailing mourners wind their way through the streets to the graveside (i.e., his "eternal home" [v. 5*b*]).

These images may be reminiscent of Barzillai's refusal to accept David's invitation to move to Jerusalem (Kidner 1976, 102). Barzillai's excuse was that he was losing his sight, taste, and hearing. He would just be a burden to David because of his failing health at eighty years of age (2 Sam. 19:34-37).

All the interpretations above of Ecclesiastes 12:2-5 lack absolute certainty; most commentators hesitate to claim just one as valid. Regardless, all seem to agree that these verses emphasize the tremendous change and loss that come with old age and death. Life seems to go downhill in old age. When a death occurs, things are never the same for the family and friends of the deceased. Gloom is a constant companion for a period.

This thought is expanded further in verses 6-7, using four metaphors for the finality of death. A severed cord, a broken bowl, a shattered pitcher, and a broken wheel cannot be repaired (v. 6). The first two probably refer to the ancient practice of hanging up oil lamps on cords before the days of electricity. When a cord that held up a lamp broke, the lamp would fall to the ground and break beyond repair. The final two metaphors refer to water pitchers and pulleys at wells and springs. Once broken, they were useless.

These metaphors reminded Qohelet's readers that there was no return to the land of the living once death occurred. Light and water, both necessary for human life, were no longer available, because the vessels used to provide them were broken. In the same way, the body decays into the dust (*'āpār*) from which it came, and the animating breath (*rûaḥ*) returns to God who gave it (Gen. 2:7; 3:19; Job 33:4; 34:14-15; Pss. 103:14; 104:29; Eccles. 3:20).

Qohelet's view of old age was quite realistic. He seemed to be writing about a time in life that he knew firsthand because he was old himself. His assessment of his senior years was summarized in Ecclesiastes 12:1: "I find no pleasure in them."

Those of us who are older can agree wholeheartedly with Qohelet's assessment. In old age, our mobility decreases. Our diet changes. Our trips to the doctor increase. Our hopes to tackle big projects disappear because we have less energy. There are more funerals to attend for our friends. The world we once knew and enjoyed seems foreign and sometimes even hostile to us. The most debilitating aspect of it all is the knowledge that things will never get better again.

As Kidner notes, in our earlier years "troubles and illnesses are chiefly set-backs, not disasters." But in old age we know that "there will be no improvement: the clouds will always gather again, and time will no longer heal, but kill" (1976, 102). Just like the severed cord, the broken bowl, the shattered pitcher, and the broken wheel, our bodies will cease to function properly someday.

Even with that knowledge, Qohelet did not wallow in self-pity. In his role as a wise teacher, he encouraged young people to be happy for as many days as they could: "Let them enjoy them all" (11:8). One can almost read between the lines a wistful longing by Qohelet to return to his youthful years.

3. Remember: God Is Central in Your Life from Beginning to End (Eccles. 12:1a)

Ecclesiastes 12:1a is a pivotal verse between the preceding verses on youth (11:7-10) and the following verses on old age and death (12:1b-7). Here Qohelet drew God into his admonitions about life. There is a critical time to recognize God as the one who brought us into being and to enter into a relationship with him. That time is during our youthful years. If we fail to make this decision at that time, we will suffer the consequences for our neglect the rest of our lives.

In one of the churches I pastored, there was a man who did not become a Christian until his late forties. Unfortunately for him, by that time his children were all grown and living on their own. On numerous occasions, he pleaded with them to come to Christ as he had, but to no avail. They had been raised as pagans and wanted to continue down that road. Almost every testimony he gave at church reflected his deep regret and sorrow that his earlier life had driven his own children away from God.

It is vitally important to introduce individuals to their Creator in their youthful years. If spiritual instruction is neglected or avoided early in life, it may never be embraced. As Davis notes, "It is unwise to assume that one can ignore God at one stage of life and 'catch up' on spiritual work at another" (2000, 224).

The word for God that Qohelet used is *bôrə'êkā* (your Creator). For centuries, scholars have been uncomfortable with this word and have proposed a number of emendations and translations (see the commentaries). However, the word makes perfect sense in this location.

The best interpretation for preaching is one by an ancient rabbi named Akabya ben Mahallalel, who lived in the first century AD. He combined three different readings of the Hebrew word: "Said the Rabbi: 'Consider three things and you will not come into the power of sin: Know whence you came [*b'rk*, "your source"]; where you are going [*bwrk*, "your pit"]; and before whom you are destined to give an accounting [*bwr'k*, "your creator"]'" (quoted in Seow 1997, 352). We cannot say for sure Qohelet had all three points in mind by his use of "your Creator," but this theology is certainly implied, and we will expand upon it below.

a. Mahallalel's phrase "whence you came" refers partially to the dust of the ground that Qohelet mentions in Ecclesiastes 12:7. This is an obvious allusion to the creation story in Genesis 2:7 where God formed a human being from the dust of the ground. It means that our bodies are made up of common elements that were here before we were. We "share in the materiality of the earth" (Lodahl 1994, 70). But the phrase also refers to the actions taken by God to change the dust into a living person. He formed the physical features of a human being and then animated this figure by breathing his breath into the creature's nostrils. By doing so, God gave humanity life.

b. Mahallalel's phrase "where you are going" points to our death. At some point in the future, life will end for each of us. Our bodies will return to the dust from whence we came, and our breath will return to God. We cannot ever escape our mortality. The only unknowns about death are *how* and *when* it will happen. For that, we have no answer. All we can say is that death is coming. Two implications derive from this thought: (1) we should make the most of our time on earth and not live foolishly (Eccles. 2:24-26; 9:7-10), and (2) we should always be prepared for death (2:15-16; 3:2; 8:7-8; 9:12).

c. Mahallalel's phrase "before whom you are destined to give an accounting" is clearly referring to God's judgment on individuals.

In most of the OT, judgment was usually associated with *a community of people*. Israel as a nation would experience God's judgment for their corporate sins. It would occur in this life, and it would be publicly known. The deportations by the Assyrians and Babylonians were two examples of God's judgment on the nation.

The wisdom literature, however, prominently emphasizes God's judgment of *individuals*. Passages such as Job 18:5-21; 38:15; Proverbs 4:18-19; 13:9; and Ecclesiastes 11:9 illustrate God's displeasure with individual wicked people and how he will deal with their sinfulness. New Testament writers continued this emphasis on individual judgment (Matt. 12:36; Rom. 1:18-32; 2:5-16; 5:12-21; 14:10-12; Heb. 4:13; 9:27; 1 Pet. 4:1-6). The main difference between the Testaments was the timing. Old Testament writers placed judgment in this life because their understanding of Sheol did not permit judgment in the next. The NT placed judgment in both this world and the afterlife, with the afterlife being the time of the final judgment.

d. The translation "your Creator" in many of our versions implies several important concepts about our relationship with God. First, it indicates that our beginning point as human beings was the result of God's desires and actions. He brought us into existence and breathed life into us. Because he wanted to do so, we must be important to him. Second, our ending point as human beings will also be the result of God's desires and actions. At some point in the future, he will remove his breath from us, thus resulting in our physical death (Eccles. 12:7). Third, the way we live our lives now should reflect our creaturely status. We are creatures and no more. Therefore, we need to act like that is our position in the universe. "Don't pretend that you are self-made or self-sufficient; you have a creator" (Davidson 1986, 84). Fourth, we are accountable to our Creator for our thoughts and actions (11:9). God wants us to live according to his plans, not ours. At the end of our lives, he will decide if we have done so.

e. The word "remember" (Eccles. 12:1) means to regain an awareness of something out of the past. As the years go by and our memories fade, we tend to forget important events that once were quite significant, such as our high school graduation, our wedding day, our first job, and the birth of our children. Sometimes, an event in the present jogs our memory of the past. We may even wish that we could go back and relive those events. We call that nostalgia.

However, OT writers were not usually thinking of nostalgia when they used the word "remember." They were usually calling on either God or the Israelites to recall the terms of the covenant and to act accordingly. Examples of Jewish leaders calling on God to remember are found in Psalm 25:6 and Jeremiah 14:21. Examples of the Lord calling on Israel to remember appear in Numbers 15:37-41 and Malachi 4:4 (3:22 HB). The point for us is that the recollection of the past should result in an impact on the present and/or the future. Remembering the covenant should lead to appreciation, actions, and renewed commitment. Commitment entails the following:

(1) A deep appreciation for the one who showed his love for us by establishing the covenant in the first place

(2) Appropriate behavioral actions that live out the terms of the covenant

(3) A renewed commitment to the one with whom we are in relationship

In Ecclesiastes 12:8, Qohelet concludes his part of the book by repeating the theme verse that appeared at the beginning (1:2). Life is complete vanity. It is like a vapor—without substance, fleeting, without value, and senseless. However, as we have seen in previous passages, Qohelet never gives up on life. There are things we can do and attitudes we can take while we are young that will make life enjoyable. The sooner we recognize that and start applying it to our own lives, the sooner we will be happy. This is Qohelet's word of hope for all who read his book.

At the same time, Qohelet wants us to keep death in mind throughout our lifespan. The awareness and acceptance of our mortality is the most important step we can take in learning how to live each day. That is why Qohelet urges his readers to go to the house of mourning rather than the house of feasting (7:2, 4). We will learn many more significant things about life in the former house than in the latter.

Qohelet's thoughts in this passage can be summarized in this way: Death is coming, but it has not yet arrived. As long as you have breath, there are still things you can do in life to bring enjoyment to

yourself and to your family. No matter how old you are, always remember to whom you belong. Focus your attention on your Creator
(12:1), not on your own problems that derive from aging or the vanity
and wickedness of life around you.

Possible Sermon Titles: "Qohelet's Advice to Young People," "An Exhortation to Young People," "Remember Your Creator," "Enjoy Life While
You Can!"

VIII. EPILOGUE AND EXCURSUS (ECCLES. 12:9-14)

Pleasing Words (Eccles. 12:9-14)

An anonymous editor wrote the final six verses in the book of Ecclesiastes (12:9-14) as concluding editorial remarks. This is clear from the change to the third person subjects and verbs.

Most likely, this editor was another sage or student of Qohelet who admired his teachings. He probably penned this epilogue within a few years of Qohelet's death.

We do not know the name of this editor. However, the person was someone who knew Qohelet well enough to be able to make an accurate description of his character and values and recognize his important contribution to Israelite wisdom literature. He describes Qohelet as wise and scholarly, as well as being an excellent teacher, writer, and thinker. The description is brief, but it gives us insight into the intellectual nature of this man.

That he took time to attach his words to the end of this book indicates that he wanted Qohelet's words to be a part of Israel's national literature. He wanted to commend this book to Israel's reading public. It was a valuable book and needed to be read and pondered.

The editor called Qohelet a "shepherd." The word "shepherd" (rō'eh) in verse 11 is modified by the word "one" ('eḥād). This has led some commentators to apply "one shepherd" to God as in Psalms 23:1; 78:52; 80:1; Isaiah 40:11; and Jeremiah 31:10. Others assumed King Solomon wrote the book and applied the term to him. This is based on the occasional appearance of "shepherd" used with other kings' names in ANE legal texts, such as the *Code of Hammurabi* ("The Prologue," i, 50 [*ANET*, 164]) and historical texts such as *The Sumerian King List* (I [*ANET*, 265-66]).

In Ecclesiastes 12:11, the editor compared the shepherd's teachings to "goads" and "nails." A goad was a prod used to get animals moving in the right direction. Nails were firmly fixed objects and, in this case, points of reference that can be counted on as conveying truth. Perhaps the nails were embedded in the prod or stick to make it sharper (Brown 2011, 117). The truth sometimes does make us uncomfortable (117) and even will "sting and provoke" (Fox 2004, 83). The instructions from wisdom teaching, therefore, should guide us in the right direction and provide true and reliable reference points.

The editor correlated the shepherd and the sages. The sages' (shepherd's) words (goads and nails) "are hard to bear but necessary for our good" (Bowes 2024, 164). More specifically, he referred to the words of "one" shepherd in particular, that is, Qohelet. His teachings were meant to prod his readers' thinking, energize their minds, and point out reliable truths as points of reference.

Shepherds care for sheep. The psalmist describes David as both a good shepherd of animals and a good shepherd of God's people, Israel, in Psalm 78:70-72. This is in stark contrast to the evil shepherds described in Jeremiah 23:1-4, who scattered the sheep. Evil shepherds do not have the sheep's best interests in mind. Ecclesiastes 12:12*a* warns against "anything in addition to" the "words of the wise" (v. 11; the sages or good shepherds). Seeking any other way in life except the way of wisdom is foolish and ruinous.

The editor concluded with traditional Jewish and foundational OT theological wisdom in verses 13-14: "Fear God and keep his commandments, for he will hold you accountable" (author's paraphrase). Qohelet and the editor had different philosophies of life. (See Bowes 2024, 170, and the sermon "How to Be Successful and Wise" in Bowes 2025, 27, to compare these differences.) These verses intentionally encourage readers to understand Qohelet's teaching within the framework of traditional OT teaching.

The words of Paul in Ephesians 5:15-17 in the NT are somewhat like those of the editor and instructions from Qohelet in Ecclesiastes. Paul admonished the church at Ephesus to live as wise people. To do so, they need to "understand what the Lord's will is" (v. 17). He instructed them to make "the most of every opportunity" (v. 16) because there was evil in the surrounding culture.

Make Lemonade

When I read Ecclesiastes as a younger man, I regarded the book as overly pessimistic and cynical about life. But the older I get, the more realistic and relevant it has become.

In my own personal life, I face increasing personal health concerns. More and more friends are passing away. There are continual ups and downs with the economic health of the nation. I have disgust at the increasing level of dishonesty and corruption in government and political parties. There is disappointment in society's failure to deal with racism, crime, and poverty. There is a failure of world leaders to abolish war as a means of settling grievances. Too many times the body of Christ has failed to live by the Golden Rule. Being overly influenced by secular politics, the church's weaknesses emerge, as we fail to address society's most pressing problems.

Our world is in a mess. Qohelet's observation that humanity does not improve although there are new discoveries and increased understanding has held true. Is life indeed vanity? If so, how can we live a meaningful life while fearing God?

One of my grandfathers was an early preacher in the American Holiness Movement. He moved around from church to church in the upper Midwest, pastoring small rural congregations in Minnesota, the Dakotas, Montana, Colorado, Nebraska, and Iowa. Times were tough, especially during the Great Depression of the 1930s. Sometimes he had to pastor a circuit of two or three churches just to keep food on his family's table.

In the late 1930s, he moved to the Los Angeles area so his oldest daughter could attend Pasadena College. Shortly after the move, he began losing his eyesight. There was nothing the doctors could do to help him. In a few years, he had to quit pastoring and go on disability. Fifteen years later, he faced another crisis when his wife developed dementia. He could not care for her because of his blindness, and so she moved into a nursing home while he went to live with relatives. After his wife died within a year, he came to live with my parents. He was sixty-seven. Outsiders might think that his life would gradually have started drifting toward death. But Grandpa was not that kind of man. He learned how to read braille and started a Christian magazine for the blind, which was eventually published by the Nazarene Publishing House.

He started writing to old friends from his college and pastoral days. Soon, he ran across a woman he had known in college. They fell in love. He taught her how to read and write braille so that they could write love letters without my parents knowing about it. Soon they were married and living in their own home. Grandpa lived another thirteen years, continuing his ministry to the blind.

Setbacks in life do not have to mean the end of the road. They can be the start of a change in life, leading to new work, new friends, and new opportunities for service to God. As our own English proverb says, "When life hands you a lemon, make lemonade."

Amid all his confusion about life's meaning, Qohelet found a way to make lemonade. He found a way to enjoy life, and he passed his recommendations along to his students and to us today.

If life has handed you a lemon, why not find a way to make something good out of it? Ask God to help you start a new chapter in your life.

Possible Sermon Titles: "Make Lemonade," "Words from the Wise Guys," "The Point Is . . . ," "The Shepherd's Prod," "Fear God and Keep His Commandments"

IX. ADDITIONAL SERMON IDEAS FROM ECCLESIASTES

Tragically, on February 4, 2023, Wendell Bowes died unexpectedly following an accident. At the time of his death, this book was still a work in progress. Qohelet correctly claimed that "of making many books there is no end, and much study wearies the body" (Eccles. 12:12). Wendell's untimely death brought an end to his writing. But his wife, Ginger, and daughter Heidi worked diligently to salvage and edit the following exegetical notes from his files, teaching notes, and lectures on Ecclesiastes. These may serve as more sketchy starters for pastors and teachers wanting to develop sermons and lessons on the unfinished chapters. Wendell's exemplary sermons on the rest of Ecclesiastes may serve as models. For further expansion, see Bowes's *The Wisdom Literature* (2024).

Wendell died before he had completed all he wanted to write about Ecclesiastes. At his family's request, I picked up the baton and have attempted to edit what he intended to publish. Now, pastors and teachers, the baton is in your hands. Take the sermon starters and his sketchy exegetical notes, collected after his death, and go preach and teach from what is one of the most challenging books in the Bible.

—George Lyons, editor

A. Religious Advice (Eccles. 5:1-9 [4:17–5:8 HB])

Verses 1-7 (4:17–5:6 HB): Advice about Religious Matters
- Obedience is more important than ritual (v. 1 [4:17 HB]).
- A few words spoken in reverence are more important than great verbosity spoken in impatience (v. 2 [5:1 HB]).
- It is better not to make a vow than to make one you cannot or will not fulfill (vv. 4-6 [3-5 HB]).

Verses 8-9 (7-8 HB): Advice about Political Matters
- Corruption in government will be punished.
- Do not get upset when you see government officials doing wrong. They will have to answer to those higher in authority.

B. The Limitations of Wealth (Eccles. 5:10–6:9 [5:9–6:9 HB])

5:10-20 (9-19 HB)
- Wealth has no inherent goodness.
- The more you have, the less you are satisfied. The law of diminishing returns applies to wealth.
- Enjoy what you have.

1. Money Can't Buy Happiness (Eccles. 5:10-12 [9-11 HB])[1]

Recall that Qohelet, the anonymous teacher responsible for Ecclesiastes, was convinced that apart from God, all human pursuits—work, success, wisdom, wealth, power, and pleasure—are vain, empty, futile, and inconsequential.

Qohelet observed that whether people had enough or not enough money, most needed and wanted more (see Eccles. 10:19). For some that craving could only be described as "love"—they preferred and pursued money above all other things. The apostle Paul claimed, "The love of money is a root of all kinds of evil" (1 Tim. 6:10). Scripture nowhere teaches that money itself is evil. The fault is not in the money, but in those who use it selfishly. Money can be used badly. And what cannot? But it can also be used well, for noble, unselfish ends (see Wesley 1760, 348-57).

Qohelet pointed out the futility of devoting the precious few days of our lives trying to accumulate more money or the things it can buy for ourselves. No matter how much we have, it is never enough. He

---

1. As Wendell's New Testament counterpart at Northwest Nazarene University for over twenty years, I knew he was the expert on the Old Testament and especially on its wisdom literature. But I learned from him and attempted to emulate his example in the Sunday school commentary I wrote for *Illustrated Bible Life* for June 18, 2023. What follows is a version of the commentary, which I wrote in January 2022. Thanks to the Foundry Publishing for granting permission to include this writing (George Lyons).

found it totally incomprehensible why anyone would worry so much about money. "This is also vanity" (Eccles. 5:10 [9 HB], KJV).

Preoccupation with money and the things it can buy is unsatisfying because the more we have, the more we need. The blessing of more children means more mouths to feed. Friends and family expect a share of our excess wealth. More cattle require more grain and pasture. Material things break and must be repaired or replaced. It costs money to defend our assets from those who might take them from us. We must hire help to care for all our stuff. Expenses increase. Some are rich "on paper" but have few liquid assets. Wealth is an elusive illusion.

Those who must engage in exhausting physical labor simply to survive sleep soundly, whether well fed or not. But wealthy aristocrats, who do almost nothing, stay awake at night worrying about protecting their overabundance and plotting how to get more. Perhaps overeating rich foods gives them both indigestion and insomnia.

2. "You Can't Take It with You" (Eccles. 5:13-17 [12-16 HB])

Conspicuously wealthy people may be despised by their envious poorer neighbors. Their conspicuous consumption makes them potential targets for desperate and violent thieves. There is one "painful reality" (Eccles. 5:13 [12 HB], AT; "grievous evil" [NIV]) of life on earth: the more people have, the more they stand to lose when disasters strike.

One bad venture (vv. 13-14 [12-13 HB]) can mean bankruptcy and the loss of everything the wealthy horded for the future. Financial ruin may come as easily by some faultless misfortune or runaway inflation as by foolish squandering. Regardless of the cause, the once-rich may have nothing left for their children to inherit. All their acquisitive ways and the worry they wasted protecting their assets are of no earthly value to anyone.

Unlike Job (1:21), Qohelet does not bless God for the leveling effect of birth and death. He simply acknowledges that all are born literally naked; all die metaphorically naked. As the old saying puts it, "You can't take it with you." How much do the rich leave when they die? They leave it all. "We enter the world with nothing, and regardless of how hard we work and how much we gain throughout life, we leave the world as we entered it, taking nothing with us" (Ogden and Zogbo 1998, 178).

Here's another "painful reality" (Eccles. 5:13 [12 HB], AT): no one takes what they earn in this world into the next. "What do people gain from all their toil on this earth?" (1:3; 3:9, author's paraphrase). Nothing.

But Qohelet's picturesque answer to that question was "a chasing after the wind" (1:14, 17). Since the Hebrew word *rûaḥ* may mean "wind," "breath," or "spirit," he may have thought of the breath of life we take at birth and give up at death. "What lasting benefit does a person have who has toiled only for his life and breath?" (Ogden and Zogbo 1998, 181). None at all!

The Hebrew in 5:17 (16 HB) says simply that people work all their days and eat in darkness. If Qohelet meant this literally, he may have had in mind workaholics or the desperate. They spent all their daylight hours working and commuting to work, with little time to enjoy the fruit of their labors (4:7-8). Twelve-hour days were the norm in antiquity (see Matt. 20:1-16). Such people did not really live while they were alive.

If this was a metaphor, Qohelet may have referred to the emotional gloom and regret of unproductive labor (see Gen. 3:17-19). People eat away their lives (Eccles. 2:23; 6:4; 11:8) with "gnawing anxiety" (5:17 [16 HB], REB). Not only must they leave everything behind at death, but also their futile pursuit of wealth meant that throughout their lives, they were angry, resentful, sick, and surrounded by people dying and mourning (Ogden and Zogbo 1998, 183). Life can be difficult. And there is no lasting satisfaction in material things.

3. So Enjoy What You Have (Eccles. 5:18-20 [17-19 HB])

Despite all of life's painful realities (Eccles. 5:10-17 [9-16 HB]), Qohelet repeatedly urged his readers to enjoy life, whatever their circumstances. Read 2:24-25; 3:12-15, 22; 5:18 (17 HB); 8:15; and 9:7-10, and note that he did not recommend pleasure for its own sake. He simply advocated accepting and enjoying life as it is, as God's gift to us. Don't fantasize about a trouble-free life! There is no such thing.

Qohelet realized that the lasting benefit of work was not accumulated wealth. We may find satisfaction in "toilsome labor" by enjoying our comparatively short lives ("few days") (5:18 [17 HB]). "Life is God's gift, and . . . we should therefore show our thankfulness by enjoying it with all its diversity, its pain and its joys" (Ogden and Zogbo 1998, 185).

The phrase "for this is their lot" explains that God rewards those who do his will with the ability to enjoy life as it is (v. 18 [17 HB]). Even interpreters from Christian traditions that advocate total abstinence acknowledge that by "drink" here, Qohelet recommended drinking wine, fermented grape juice (2:3; 9:7; 10:19). But he totally rejected drunkenness as folly (2:3; 10:17; see Prov. 20:1; 21:17; 23:20-21, 30-31; Rom. 13:13; 1 Cor. 5:11; 6:10; Gal. 5:21; Eph. 5:18). Nevertheless, in cultures (like ours) in which few practice moderation, we might disagree and consider teetotalism the better option.

Beyond the material gifts God gives, as he sees fit, he also enables us to accept life as it is and to enjoy his good gifts (Eccles. 6:2). Perhaps heartfelt gratitude is God's best gift. People have little time to worry about their lives when God keeps them busy enjoying life.[2]

6:1-6: Money and Misery

The person who has all things—wealth, honor, a large family, a long life—but does not enjoy them is living a miserable life. It is vanity. That person would have been better off to be stillborn. He or she would have only known darkness. As it is, that person has seen the light but now lives in darkness. This is already mentioned in Proverbs 4:23 and in Job 3.

The quality of one's life is more important than its quantity. Many days of life cannot compensate for mostly lifeless days. If you live two thousand years and have one hundred children and cannot enjoy life, you are most miserable. Jesus wisely observed that "life does not consist in an abundance of possessions" (Luke 12:15).

6:7-9: Never Enough

- People are never content with what they have but constantly strive for more.

---

2. George Lyons's comments end here.

- What you see in real life is better than what you desire and cannot see.
- A modern proverb is similar: "A bird in the hand is worth two in the bush."

C. Miscellaneous Proverbs (Eccles. 6:10–7:14)

6:10-12: Living in the Dark

These verses emphasize the sovereignty of God. Human freedom is limited at best. God has already named everything—that is, he has everything under control. We would do well not to enter into a dispute with one who is stronger than we are (especially God). Who really knows what is good for us? We are in the dark about much in life.

7:1-14: This Is Better than That

The form of this section resembles Proverbs. These are short, condensed sayings grouped around common themes. Seven of these sayings use the "better than" formula (comparisons). The sayings often refer to opposites, playing one off another.

v. 1a: A good name is better than the costliest item you can imagine. See Proverbs 22:1, where it is compared to riches.

vv. 1b, 2, 4: Death is better than birth. Qohelet is referring to the death of another person, not himself (see v. 2b, which refers to attending a funeral as a guest, not being the memorialized person there). Death is a great teacher about life. One learns much more from death than from partying. What can we learn from death? The shortness of life, our priorities, models of faith and goodness, and God's goodness over many years.

v. 3: In the same way, sorrow is a great teacher.

vv. 5-6: Rebuke from a wise person is better than songs or praise from a fool. The fool's words do not mean anything. Consider the source. He cannot teach us anything. Qohelet likens the laugh of a fool to the crackling of twigs in a fire.

v. 7: Oppression and bribes are corrupt. Here Qohelet speaks of activities that might lead a usually wise person away from good behavior into folly. Oppression and a bribe can be understood as pressure and enticement. These are probably the chief reasons why politicians become corrupt.

v. 8: Better is the end of a thing. Hindsight is better than foresight. This seems to be a common wisdom theme.

v. 9: Do not be quick to anger (cited in James 1:19).

vv. 11-12: Be aware of the importance and advantage of wisdom.

v. 13: God's decisions are permanent. We cannot change what he desires to happen.

v. 14: Accept what you are given when it comes, whether good times or bad.

Introduction to Sunday School Lesson on Ecclesiastes 7:1-14[3]

Ecclesiastes 7:1-12 addresses the question raised in 6:12*a*: "Who knows what is good for a person" during their "few and meaningless days . . . ?" Ecclesiastes 7:13-14 answers the question in 6:12*b*: "Who can tell them what will happen . . . after they are gone?"

The epilogue of Ecclesiastes (12:9-14) helps explain how such a pessimistic book was included in the canon of Holy Scripture: apart from God, all human pursuits—work, success, wisdom, wealth, power, and pleasure—are vain, empty, futile, and inconsequential.

Like Qohelet, the apostle Paul considered death the universal destiny of sinful humanity (Rom. 1:18–3:20). But by faith in the saving work of Christ (3:21–11:36), God mercifully offers eternal life instead. So Paul urged Christians to offer themselves fully to the service of God (12:1-2).

---

3. What follows is a portion of the Sunday school commentary I wrote for *Illustrated Bible Life* for June 4, 2023. Thanks to the Foundry Publishing for granting permission to include this version, which I wrote in January 2022 (George Lyons).

1. Human Life Is a Terminal Illness (Eccles. 7:1-4)

Following fleeting fame is futile. Preoccupation with the praise of people is counterproductive. Like perfume, fame's scent is short lived. Given the brevity of life, it is wise to find contentment in every moment God gives (Eccles. 2:24-26; 3:12, 22; 5:18-19 [17-18 HB]; 6:3-6; 8:15; 9:7-10). Only at death may the lasting legacy of one's true character be assessed (see 7:8). But eulogies are for funerals, not birthday celebrations.

Qohelet used sarcasm to warn "that an unhealthy desire for fame is to wish for one's own death" (Bennett 2010, 122). But we should take seriously his sobering reminder: All humans are mortal. We all have expiration dates. No one leaves this world alive. We all have a terminal diagnosis. For some, the time of the end is just sooner rather than later.

On the subject of death, Qohelet could offer no good news (see Eccles. 3:18-21). "Who knows" whether there is anything after death (v. 21)? Christians know that the resurrection of Jesus Christ offers "a living hope" (1 Pet. 1:3). Christ shared in our humanity to free us from the "fear of death" (Heb. 2:14-15).

The claim here that "sorrow" (NIV[1984]) or "frustration is better than laughter" is wholly out of character with the rest of Ecclesiastes (Eccles. 7:3). Thus it appears that Qohelet again resorted to sarcasm (see 1:18; 7:2). But his reminder to take life seriously must not be ignored. We should sorrow over the suffering and injustice in our crooked world (7:13). Life is not a party. Even our own "suffering can bring a depth of character . . . missing in those who have only known frivolity (see 2:2; Prov 14:13)" (Bennett 2010, 122). The apostle Paul affirmed that "suffering produces perseverance; perseverance, character; and character, hope" (Rom. 5:3-4).

Wisdom calls us to live with the sobering awareness of our own mortality. We live in perishable bodies. Every day we live from birth on, we are dying. It is wise to realize that for most (so-called) middle-aged adults, things will get a whole lot worse before they get a whole lot better. Nevertheless, for Christians, life is not over when it's over. Our true lives have only begun in earnest. It is suicidal folly to live for pleasure alone, flippantly denying the inevitability of death. Sadly, even some professing Christians live this way (Phil. 3:18-21).

2. Wisdom vs. Folly (Eccles. 7:5-7)

The mindless songs of "the house of pleasure" (Eccles. 7:4) desensitized fools to the depressing reality of death. Fools disdained "rebuke" (v. 5; see Prov. 12:1). They found reprimand, sage advice, and constructive criticism annoying. No one could tell them what to do. The pleasures of the moment blinded them to their coming destruction (Eccles. 7:6).

Like stereotypical adolescents, fools make no plans, give no thought to the consequences of their actions, and lack impulse control. Fools smirk at the prospect of death, imagining they are invincible exceptions. "Death? Not me! Not anytime soon." Their songs distract them from the harsh reality of their mortality. Qohelet's warning about the inevitability of death (vv. 1-4) was a wake-up call for such fools.

English translations cannot capture the original wordplay in verses 5 and 6. The words "song," "crackling," "fools," and "pot" in Hebrew are similar in sound. Dried "thorns" made good kindling only. The sizzle of their hot but brief flame and its noise (Ps. 118:12; Joel 2:5) soon fizzle out. Thorns are useless for cooking. The silly songs of fools are similarly "meaningless" (Eccles. 7:6). Like thorns, fools will be destroyed.

The clear point here is that even wisdom has its limits. But difficulties translating and interpreting Ecclesiastes 7:7 allow for several possible meanings:

- "Extortion" (threats of violence) or "bribes" (promises of benefits; see Exod. 23:8; Prov. 15:27; 21:14) may cloud the judgment of the wise. Coercion and corruption turn "a wise person" into a "fool" and make their advice worthless.
- A supposedly "wise person" who takes advantage of others is actually a "fool."
- A "wise" person who tolerates "oppression" (NRSV's translation of the Hebrew word rendered "extortion" here) in society not only is foolish but also threatens the survival of the community.

3. Living between Past and Future (Eccles. 7:8-10)

Qohelet warned that pessimism about the present was folly: don't undervalue the present with unrealistic future dreams or flawed, overly rosy memories of an idyllic past that never actually existed.

Ecclesiastes 7:8-9 expands on verse 1. Death is "the end" of life; birth, "its beginning" (v. 8). Qohelet was offering this advice: Don't wish your lives away by being overly anxious for the recognition that comes only at death. Accomplishment and excellence in most life endeavors require patience and practice. Saints, sages, and superstars are made, not born. It takes a lifetime to cultivate the kind of character one can take justified pride in. But you can't be sure how others will assess you after you've died (see 6:12).

There are changing seasons in every life—"a season for every activity under the heavens" (3:1). Not only the time between being born and dying calls for patience. There is also the time between planting and harvesting, demolition and rebuilding, and so forth (see 3:2-8). "In between" times complicate life. Waiting is difficult.

The Hebrew words translated "patience" and "pride" are literally "long in spirit" and "high in spirit" respectively (7:8). The opposite, forbidden response to patiently waiting for "the end" (v. 8) is to "be quickly provoked in . . . spirit" (v. 9). Growing angry is a totally unproductive inward response to circumstances. Anger brings only sorrow, grief, and frustration (1:18; 2:23; 5:2, 17 [1, 16 HB]; 7:3). To encourage "anger" is as foolish as spoiling a misbehaving child in your "lap" (7:9; see Prov. 14:33).

The so-called good old days exist only in our flawed, selective memories. Millennia ago it was "not wise" to ask, "Why were the old days better than these?" (Eccles. 7:10). Now, it is even more foolish: "The truth is that people today on average are faring much better than they were at any point in history" (Vincent 2019). Learn to appreciate this moment—today. (Consider the lyrics of Bill and Gloria Gaither's "We Have This Moment, Today" [1975].)

4. Life-Giving Wisdom (Eccles. 7:11-12)

Qohelet had serious misgivings about wealth (Eccles. 5). But he acknowledged that material resources ("money" and/or "an inheritance") offer generational "benefits" for earthly life ("those who see the sun") (7:11-12; see 1:3, 9, 13; 3:1, 16; 6:12). And wisdom has its limits (see 7:7). But, together, wisdom and wealth are "good" (v. 11); they provide those who have them essential security (v. 12; "shelter" [NIV] or "protection" [NASB, NRSV]). Money may provide a family with food and shelter. But wisdom enables them truly to live while they are alive (see Prov 16:22). Only the "knowledge" of "wisdom preserves those who have it" (Eccles. 7:12).

5. Consider Creation (Eccles. 7:13-14)

Wisdom calls for humans to find satisfaction in God's gifts in the present. Compared to God, human power and wisdom are ineffective, inconsequential, and sorely limited.

We need to reflect on "what God has done"—God's role as all-powerful Creator (Eccles. 7:13; see 3:11, 14; 8:17). God is ultimately responsible for all that exists—both good and bad. Qohelet focused on the created world as it now exists: "crooked"—twisted and bent (7:13; see 1:15). He did not distinguish what God actively did and what God only allowed.

Qohelet's rhetorical question in 7:13 implies that humans are powerless to change the world. His failure to consider intermediate causes may echo Yahweh's response to Moses's objection that his speech defect disqualified him from accepting God's call to deliver Israel from Egypt (read Exod. 4:11-12). God can do what humans cannot. Paul explained that the fallen state of creation was caused by human rebellion against God. But God will restore creation to its pristine goodness when human redemption is complete (Rom. 8:18-25).

People cannot change reality: there are "good" and "bad" times in every life (Eccles. 7:14). Happiness is the appropriate response "when times are good" (v. 14; see 2:24; 3:12-13, 22). Because humans cannot know the future, they should not complain "when times are bad" (7:14; see 1:13; 5:13 [12 HB]; 6:1). In difficult circumstances, wisdom calls us to "consider this" (7:14): What is God up to now? What can we learn from this? "You never know what is going to happen next" (v. 14, GNT). Paul was confident that "in all things God works for the good of those who love him" (Rom. 8:28).[4]

---

4. George Lyons's comments end here.

D. The Golden Mean and the Lack of Wisdom (Eccles. 7:15-29)

7:15-18: The Golden Mean

Qohelet observes that sometimes the righteous die early and the wicked live to old age. Therefore, one should not go to extremes of either righteousness or wickedness, for it may not get you anywhere. It is better to seek a moderate, middle course—the golden mean. Righteousness here probably refers to "overly righteous" legalists, like the Pharisees. In other words, do not seek one or the other, thinking that you will get something out of it, because the pathway does not always turn out as you think it should.

7:19-25: The Lack of Wisdom

Wisdom is of great value and gives strength to people, but humanity is basically weak. People sin, curse, and have a hard time understanding life. Ecclesiastes 7:20 is similar to Romans 3:23.

7:26-29: Wisdom Is Rare

One should avoid a woman with loose morals (see sermon "Lady Foolishness Has Her Eyes on You" in Bowes 2025, 65). Qohelet sounds as if he has taken a poll of people to discover wisdom about life. Here is the result: wisdom is rarely found in human beings. However, all humanity has gone astray from the Creator's plan. The odds here are not too great for either men or women.

E. Living Under Authority and with Injustice (Eccles. 8:1-17)

8:1-9: Looking Wise

v. 1: This section begins with a wisdom saying: wisdom even affects one's looks. The wise person is truly confident that he or she is on the right path, and that confidence is noticeable on his or her countenance. Again, this emphasizes wisdom.

Wisdom is the highest good in the mind of the sages, but there are still problems with it. Wisdom does not solve every issue or give every answer a person needs; nevertheless, it is the best thing out there.

Qohelet offers sound reasons for striving to be a good citizen, which meant obeying the king:

v. 2: "You took an oath." This may be referring to the coronation ceremony when a king began his reign. The people promised that they would be good citizens.

vv. 3-4: The king can do "whatever he pleases" (v. 3). This was written for a monarchical context. In a democracy, there are checks and balances and the leader cannot do anything he wants. Doing whatever one pleases has caused many people in high places to fall.

v. 5: It will go well for you. Common sense tells you that obeying the law will bring you better results than breaking the law. Even the king is subject to the law. He, too, is subject to the same limitations as others. He must experience death and beware of war. Further, he can never bottle up the "spirit of humanity" (AT) or the "wind" (v. 8).

v. 8: There is no way to divert death or delay it. It comes to all. Qohelet wished it did not.

8:10-15: Sometimes Things Don't Go as Expected

As a general principle, Qohelet believed that God rewarded righteousness and punished wickedness. However, it did not always work out that way in practical experience. Sometimes the wicked were buried with great pomp and ceremony. Many mobsters today have great funerals.

Sometimes punishment did not speedily follow a crime, and young people thought that the evil person had gotten away with it. Thus they also sought to live a life of wickedness. Still, justice eventually catches up with everyone, and it is better to fear God.

This is a major problem for law enforcement. Too many people get away with their crimes, and too many have justice delayed. Legal systems with numerous opportunities for appeal can protect criminals. This defeats the whole moral tone of the government. In difficult times, it is no surprise that a lot of people turn to crime. How would it affect the crime rate if every person who committed a crime knew in advance that they would be caught within a month and start facing their punishment?

True, the righteous sometimes suffer and the wicked sometimes do well. This is vanity; it does not make sense. The best course of action is to enjoy what you have and not worry about the injustices in life. This is the same thought that Qohelet mentions in Ecclesiastes 6:1-6.

8:16-17: Impossible

Qohelet claims that he tried to figure out the ways of life, but it was impossible. Some may claim to know them, but they really do not. No one knows the mind of God (see Job 15:8; Isa. 40:13-14; Jer. 23:18; Rom. 11:34). Qohelet emphasizes that we all need a good dose of humility. This pulls the rug out from under every egocentric person who has ever lived.

F. More Miscellaneous Proverbs (Eccles. 10:1-20)

v. 1: Just as a dead fly ruins a whole bottle of perfume, so one fool can undo a great deal of wisdom.

v. 2: Wisdom and folly are two very different pathways.

v. 3: Even when fools are on the right pathway, they still act like a fools.

v. 4: Stay at your post, even if your ruler or boss is angry with you. This admonition may testify to your superior of the faithfulness you bring to your work. And it encourages a good work ethic.

vv. 5-7: Among the inequities of life are a slave on horseback and princes on foot. Life does not always work out as we expect. Remember the tortoise and the hare (9:11-12). Sometimes life is topsy-turvy. Jesus observed, "The last will be first, and the first will be last" (Matt. 20:16).

vv. 8-9: Dangers are inherent in various activities: digging a pit to trap an animal, breaking down a wall around a field, quarrying stone, and splitting logs. Every activity has a potential for danger. It may not work out as you had planned. Life is always uncertain.

vv. 10-11: Even when you are cautious, there may be troublesome outcomes. For example, it is a good idea to sharpen the axe head before beginning to chop wood. It is a good idea to charm a deadly snake before getting near it.

vv. 12-15: The characteristics of fools are as follows:
- Endless talking that ends in wicked madness.
- They think they know the future, but no one does.
- Their labors exhaust them.
- They have no sense of direction in life; they do not even know the way to town.

vv. 16-17: A land that has a child or servant for a king or whose leaders party and get drunk is in for trouble.

v. 18: Failure to keep up with proper house maintenance will lead to trouble. In other words, "Be prepared" (motto of the Boy Scouts). These may be a subtle political comment about Israel's leadership.

v. 19: This may be a positive comment on enjoying life. But it may be a subtle political comment about leaders who spend too much time partying.

v. 20: Be careful what you say about others behind their backs. It may get back to them. The same applies today with posts online; they stay there forever.

G. Giving (Eccles. 11:1-6)

v. 1: Being generous will benefit you. An anonymously generous man said recently, "Anyone who says money can't buy happiness has never given anything away."

v. 2: Give of your means to others while you can, for disaster may take it all away tomorrow. This advice may encourage a diversified investment portfolio.

v. 3: The rain and the wind do whatever they want whenever they want; they are beyond human control.

v. 4: The farmer who waits for the weather to be just right will never grow a crop.

v. 5: The mysterious nature of God is compared to the mystery about how life is given to a baby in its mother's womb.

v. 6: Have a good work ethic. Be ready to work in the morning or evening.

APPENDIX A
ALPIN WENDELL BOWES
NOVEMBER 6, 1945–FEBRUARY 4, 2023

Alpin Wendell Bowes was born on November 6, 1945, in San Francisco, California, to Rev. Alpin P. and Betty J. Bowes, who were pastoring a new home mission Church of the Nazarene. This was their first pastorate after graduating from Pasadena College in the early 1940s. Three years later the family moved to a new pastorate in Reedley, California. They were only in Reedley for a few months before Wendell's father was asked to become the office manager of the newly created Department of Home Missions and Evangelism at the Nazarene Headquarters in Kansas City, Missouri.

The family moved to Prairie Village, Kansas, and began attending the Rainbow Boulevard Church of the Nazarene and, later, Nall Avenue Church. Wendell's father served for twenty-one years in the Department of Home Missions and then took a position at the Nazarene Publishing House as director of sales for another twelve years.

Wendell's mother was also heavily involved in denominational church ministries. She worked for several years as a secretary in the office of the general superintendents. Then she was asked to become the editor of Cradle Roll and children's church materials in the Department of Church Schools. She worked there for about eighteen years and then completed nine years as the office manager for the district superintendent of the Kansas City District. Both parents were active in their local church, serving on the church board, teaching Sunday school classes, singing in the choir, and contributing to the missionary society.

Wendell was the last in a line of four Alpins in the Bowes family. He grew up as the oldest in a family of three boys with Bradley and Kenneth.

Prairie Village, Kansas, was one of the rapidly expanding suburbs of Kansas City following World War II. New schools were being built every year to accommodate the expanding population. As a result, Wendell attended four elementary schools in his first three years of school—Prairie, Porter, Highlands, and Belinder. He went to Indian Hills Junior High and Shawnee Mission East High School, where he graduated in 1963. One of his favorite courses was the marching band, where he played the trumpet. At their home church, Wendell and Brad sat in the front pew every Sunday evening and played their trumpet and trombone with the congregational singing.

Wendell began to sense his personal need of God about the age of ten. He was saved at a revival meeting in his home church about this time. Shortly after, he began to recognize God's calling into ministry. This was confirmed through a school project in junior high where he was required to create a notebook on a possible career. He chose the ministry as his career and interviewed a couple of pastors to get their perspective. He learned that a minister's job "is to bring God to people and people to God." This was Wendell's driving force behind his whole life's work.

Wanting to strike out on his own, Wendell traveled far from home to Nampa, Idaho, to attend Northwest Nazarene College (NNC). There he majored in philosophy-religion and was much influenced by Dr. Joseph Mayfield, Dr. Elwood Sanner, and Dr. Morris Weigelt. He spent his junior year at British Isles Nazarene College (BINC), now Nazarene Theological College in Manchester, England, where he came to admire the scholarship of Dr. Alex Deasley. He also took two courses from the renowned Dr. F. F. Bruce at the University of Manchester. That year in England was eye-opening because it introduced him to other cultures and life experiences. It profoundly affected his later passion for encouraging college students to spend a semester in another country. The British style of preaching also caught his attention and guided his own attempts at preaching in later years.

Before going to BINC, Wendell started dating an elementary education major named Virginia (also known as Ginger). They met in speech class. Neither one was very comfortable in delivering speeches, yet both later entered vocations that called for constant speaking abilities. Wendell prayed many times about his speaking skills until God promised him one day, "He would never put [him] in a place where [he] would be embarrassed because of [his] lack of speaking skills." Wendell trusted him and God fulfilled his promise over and over again as he used Wendell's preaching to bring people to the Lord.

Wendell and Ginger's romance continued through letter writing while Wendell was in England. They were married in Spokane, Washington, after Wendell's graduation.

Wendell graduated magna cum laude from NNC in 1967 with a bachelor of arts degree in philosophy-religion. He was inducted into Phi Delta Lambda, the Nazarene honor society. The couple then moved to Kansas City to attend Nazarene Theological Seminary, where Wendell graduated cum laude in 1970 with a master of divinity degree. He then attended Princeton Theological Seminary in Princeton, New Jersey, for a year, where he received the master of theology degree in New Testament studies in 1971. Dr. Bruce Metzger was a great mentor who showed him scholarly ways of studying the Bible while maintaining a Christlike spirit.

At that point Wendell felt the Lord leading him into the pastorate in order to gain some practical experience in ministry. He became a third-generation pastor in the Church of the Nazarene. His first pastorate was at Port Elizabeth, New Jersey, on the Philadelphia District, followed by pastorates at Bristol and Selinsgrove, Pennsylvania. Each was approximately three and a half years in length. He was ordained at the 1973 Philadelphia District Assembly by Dr. Orville W. Jenkins.

Each of his pastorates was in a different demographic community. Port Elizabeth was a rural spot along the main highway between Philadelphia and Cape May, New Jersey. The town had about two hundred houses up and down the highway. They traveled eight miles into Millville to buy gasoline. They started a bus ministry while there, and the church grew from an average of 100 to 130. His second pastorate at Bristol was in an older Italian Catholic suburb of row houses to the northeast of Philadelphia. There were more people within two blocks of their church in Bristol than there were within two miles in Port Elizabeth. The church there also grew during his ministry. His third pastorate in Selinsgrove was a small college town in central Pennsylvania. Again, they used a bus ministry and an active church program to expand attendance. The people there had a strong sense of the importance of evangelism, and about 250 people per year responded to Wendell's preaching and altar calls.

In 1974 while still pastoring full time, Wendell began a doctoral program at Dropsie College in Philadelphia. His major was ancient Near Eastern studies, with minors in Bible and cognate languages. His classes included the history, cultures, religions, and languages of the ancient Near East. He took courses in a dozen languages. His thirteen-hundred-page dissertation was titled "A Theological Study of Old Babylonian Personal Names." After thirteen years, he finally graduated in 1987 with a PhD.

In 1982, Wendell accepted an offer from NNC (now Northwest Nazarene University, or NNU) to become professor of Old Testament. This began a twenty-nine-year career of teaching young people how to use and love the Bible. This was especially challenging as he discovered most students knew little about the OT and regarded it as secondary to the NT. Wendell's teaching load included all of the OT courses at NNU, both at the undergraduate and graduate levels, as well as the freshman Biblical Literature course, and courses in Biblical Hebrew, NT Greek, and ancient Near Eastern history and culture. He had two opportunities to teach courses to pastors and church leaders in Johannesburg, South Africa, and the Far East.

He developed an active interest in biblical archaeology, lecturing many times on this topic at NNU and in churches of the Treasure Valley. He participated in three archaeological digs at Tall al-'Umayri, Jordan. For many years he coordinated NNU's study-abroad program at Jerusalem University College in Israel and on two occasions took groups of students with him. He also produced several archaeological displays in the lobby of NNU's Williams Hall that illustrated the contribution of archaeology to biblical studies.

In 1990, he was selected by the National Endowment for the Humanities to attend an eight-week summer seminar at Yale University titled "The Bible in the Light of Cuneiform Literature." This experience resulted in a book chapter on kingship in ancient Israel and Mesopotamia.

In addition to teaching, Wendell was deeply involved in the administration of the Religion Department at NNU, serving as chair of the department for eighteen years and director of the master of ministry program for eleven years. Through his efforts NNU developed the most thorough and creative curriculum in the area of ministerial studies of any Nazarene college at that time. He also served on many faculty committees and chaired several of them. In 2004, he was elected by the faculty to a two-year term as Chair of the Faculty. He also served two terms as president and vice president of Phi Delta Lambda, the Nazarene honor society. Wendell retired in 2011 after having taught over six thousand students. At that time, NNU granted him emeritus status.

One of the reasons Wendell retired when he did was to answer God's calling to a writing ministry. This was something he had wanted to do for a long time, but the demands of teaching prevented him from giving it much time. Wendell's writings now include over twenty-five articles in the adult Nazarene Sunday school curriculum. He also wrote the "Study Notes on the Book of Job" for the NIV *Reflecting God Study Bible*. He contributed chapters to several books and finished a full-length commentary on the book of Job in the New Beacon Bible Commentary series. A second book, *Consider My Servant Job* on preaching from Job, appeared in 2021. *The Wisdom Literature* in the Reading and Interpreting the Bible Series was released in 2024. The fourth and fifth books, released in 2025, were companion volumes—*Half Full*, on Proverbs, and *Half Empty*, on Ecclesiastes, which was nearly complete at the time of his death.

He was a longtime member of three scholarly societies—the Society of Biblical Literature, the American Schools of Oriental Research, and the National Association of Professors of Hebrew. His honors included Outstanding Young Men of America, Who's Who in Religion, Who's Who Among America's Teachers, and Who's Who in America.

When Wendell and Ginger first moved to Nampa in 1982, they decided to help out in some of the smaller Nazarene churches in the Treasure Valley. Wherever they attended, whether in the pastorate or during his teaching career, Wendell taught an adult Sunday school class for over thirty years. For the last seventeen years at Nampa College Church, he created his own Sunday school curriculum each Sunday that focused on books in the OT. He had a passion for helping people understand the OT, whether through Sunday school, college classes, or writing. Approximately 75 percent of the chapters in the OT were covered by his faithful Sunday school teaching.

Even after leaving the active pastorate, Wendell continued to preach occasionally, both in NNU's chapel services and in churches of various denominations in the Treasure Valley. While pastoring and later while teaching, Wendell was a member of the Philadelphia and Intermountain District Boards of Ministerial Studies for about fifteen years.

Few knew the extent of his accomplishments. Most knew him as a humble servant of Christ, with the potential for surprising injections of dry humor in any conversation. His childhood mischief matured into a fun-loving man who loved to learn and understand new things. Calm, respectful, organized, wise, patient, gentle, stable, and faithful were his next most commonly described attributes. He loved his family, and they experienced his love in countless ways. In retirement, his hobbies expanded to include model trains, gardening, and jigsaw puzzles.

Wendell and Ginger were married for fifty-five years. In addition to his wife and two brothers, Wendell is survived by two daughters—Heidi Bowes and Shelley Getty. Heidi is a missionary with the Church of the Nazarene. Shelley is married to Rev. John Getty, and they have two children—Simon and Johonah. Shelley is a math professor, and John is a Nazarene pastor.

APPENDIX B

TRUST GOD

A Sermon Prepared by George Lyons
for the Memorial Service of A. Wendell Bowes
on February 18, 2023

It has been my sad privilege to preach at far too many funerals. Most were for friends in the Whosoever Sunday school class, which I taught here at College Church for over twenty years. And most of these were at least twenty years my senior.

I never expected to speak at the funeral honoring the memory of my young friend and colleague, Wendell Bowes. I say "young" because he was just a couple of years older than I. What can a has-been New Testament professor say befitting an extraordinarily gifted Old Testament scholar and saintly man? I'll attempt to do so, to honor Wendell's last request.

Before I met Wendell personally for the first time in 1991, I felt I already knew him. The names of his parents, Alpin and Betty Bowes, appeared regularly in Nazarene Sunday school literature while I was growing up. Wendell's paternal grandfather was a significant leader in the first generation of Nazarene preachers. Wendell honorably contributed to the rich legacy of his godly heritage.

The older I get, the more I realize that my "conversion" at age five is far less responsible for the person I am than the family into which I was born. My maternal grandmother's conversion at a tent revival in the 1920s, when she was in her thirties, decisively changed the trajectory of my entire family. She had only a second grade education, but the costly decision she and my grandfather made to entrust their lives

117

to God and to stake their lot with the Church of the Nazarene have shaped my family for nearly a century—four generations.

I am the undeserving recipient of God's steadfast love, which he promised to extend to "a thousand generations of those who love him and keep his commandments" (Deut. 7:9). Wendell believed that the sacred trust he had received and preserved would continue to shape his family, long after his death. A thousand generations is well over twenty thousand years. Get your mind around that, if you can.

But Wendell asked me not to say much about him. He wanted me to encourage you, especially his family, to continue the legacy of trusting God that he received. Wendell's part of the race is now complete. The baton is in your hand. Don't drop it! You are recipients of a priceless heritage. Keep trusting God.

God called and commissioned Joshua the son of Nun, Moses's assistant, not his son, to be his successor, with these words in Deuteronomy 31:23: "Be strong and bold, for you shall bring the Israelites into the land that I promised them; *I will be with you*" (NRSV; italics added). But Deuteronomy 34:9 notes that "Joshua son of Nun was full of the spirit of wisdom, because Moses had laid his hands on him" (NRSV).

One of Wendell's favorite biblical texts was the opening verses of Joshua 1:

After the death of Moses the servant of the LORD, the LORD spoke to Joshua son of Nun, Moses' assistant, saying, "My servant Moses is dead. Now proceed to cross the Jordan . . . into the land that I am giving to . . . the Israelites. Every place that the sole of your foot will tread upon I have given to you, as I promised to Moses. . . . No one shall be able to stand against you all the days of your life. *As I was with Moses, so I will be with you*; I will not fail you or forsake you. Be strong and courageous . . . , being careful to act in accordance with all the law that my servant Moses commanded you . . . so that you may be successful wherever you go. . . . For then you shall make your way prosperous, and then you shall be successful. I hereby command you: Be strong and courageous; do not be frightened or dismayed, for *the LORD your God is with you* wherever you go." (vv. 1-9, NRSV; italics added)

The three-times repeated command to be strong and courageous reenforced how urgent it was for Joshua to trust God's promises to Moses and their ancestors. Trust in the face of significant challenges and opposition requires considerable strength and courage. The necessary resource Joshua needed to fulfill his divine calling was the assurance, "As I was with Moses, so I will be with you" (v. 5, NRSV).

What did that mean? What would it involve for God to be with Joshua as he was with Moses? Certainly, Joshua did not imagine he was to be a competitor of Moses. God did not expect Joshua to exceed Moses's unique accomplishments. Deuteronomy 34 insists, "Never since has there arisen a prophet in Israel like Moses, whom the LORD knew face to face. He was unequaled for all the signs and wonders that the LORD sent him to perform in the land of Egypt . . . and for all the mighty deeds and all the terrifying displays of power that Moses performed in the sight of all Israel" (vv. 10-12, NRSV).

Joshua's assignment was different from Moses's, but equally significant. Nevertheless, the book of Joshua mentions some remarkable parallels: Moses sent spies into the promised land (Num. 13; Deut. 1); Joshua sent spies into the city of Jericho (Josh. 2). Moses led the people safely across the Red Sea (Exod. 14); Joshua led Israel across the Jordan River at flood stage (Josh. 3). God encountered Moses in a burning bush with the command, "Remove the sandals from your feet, for the place on which you are standing is holy ground" (Exod. 3:5, NRSV); the enigmatic commander of the Lord's army gave Joshua the same command (Josh. 5:15).

The same God who equipped Moses to accomplish what God had called him to do similarly worked in the life of Joshua, his successor. For both, trusting God involved more than simply believing God existed.

Trust is not only individual; it is communal and generational. It required the infant Moses's parents to risk defying Pharaoh's orders and hide their son. Even Pharaoh's daughter, who found the baby floating in the Nile, unwittingly helped prepare Moses to be God's agent of deliverance, complete with a full-ride scholarship at the Egyptian University of Imperial Administration. Pharaoh's decree, intended to destroy all the male children of Israelite slaves, phenomenally backfired. But the journey from slavery to freedom was long, arduous, complicated, and fraught with potential disasters along the way. An entire generation of whining Israelites died in the wilderness not a hundred miles from the promised land, because they refused to trust God. Israel's exodus from Egypt happened under the leadership of Moses only because *God was with him*. God enabled Moses to do what he could not do in his own strength.

For God to be "with" Moses involved more than merely being passively present as an unseen spectator of all Moses did on his own. God is not just an always-present, ever-supportive helicopter parent who shows up at all his children's sporting events, piano recitals, parent-teacher conferences, and so forth. God is not just an encouraging cheerleader on the sidelines.

My dad was a superior high school athlete, lettering in several sports. I, on the other hand, am a total klutz. To please Dad, I tried out for the freshman softball team. In my tiny high school, it took no talent to make the team; to play was another matter. I faithfully attended practice and sat on the bench during every game. All our games were immediately after school, so Dad, because of his work schedule, could not attend. But one game day he surprised me. He left work early to come watch my game—to be *with me*. Of course, I was on the bench. But, to my surprise, the coach must have noticed Dad's presence and decided to put me in as a relief pitcher. I loaded the bases and walked in the winning run. Frankly, I would rather Dad had missed that game. Not long after that, I ran across Dad's high school report cards. He was a solid C student. I knew I could do better than that. So I abandoned sports to become a serious student. Athletic failure partially explains why I'm here today.

God's presence with us is not just a matter of passively being there to watch us fail at our feeble efforts. God actively enables us to do successfully what he gifted and called us to do. As our Creator, he leads us and assists us as we follow his guidance. When we trust God to accomplish his purposes for us, he gives us the fulfilling life he wants us to experience.

Because God was with Joshua, Joshua was enabled to lead Israel's conquest of the promised land, which Moses never reached. You have heard the opening words of the book of Joshua, God's promise to be *with Joshua as he was with Moses.* Hear now the rest of the story from the last two chapters of the book:

> A long time afterward, when the LORD had given rest to Israel . . . and Joshua was old and well advanced in years, Joshua summoned all Israel . . . and said to them, "*I am now old and well advanced in years*; and you have seen *all that the LORD your God has done* to all these nations for your sake, for it is *the LORD your God* who has fought for you. . . . One of you puts to flight a thousand, since it is *the LORD your God who fights for you,* as he promised you. Be very careful, therefore, to *love the LORD your God. . . .*
>
> "And now I am about to go the way of all the earth, and you know in your hearts and souls, all of you, that *not one thing has failed of all the good things that the LORD your God promised* concerning you; all have come to pass for you, not one of them has failed. . . .
>
> ". . . [But] it was not by your sword or by your bow. *[God] gave you [the] land. . . .*
>
> "Now therefore *revere the LORD, and serve him* in sincerity and in faithfulness. . . . Choose this day whom you will serve . . . ; but as for me and my household, we will serve the LORD." (Josh. 23.1-3, 10-11, 14; 24:12-15, NRSV; italics added)

God has not called us to be superheroes. He has called us to trust him to do the humanly impossible. He has called us to love, worship, and serve him—to let him be the foundation and center of our lives.

God has not called us to be successful in the world's eyes. But as we allow God to use us to accomplish his purposes in this world, his presence and power assure our success in the opinion of the only one whose opinion really matters.

God promises to be with those who accept his invitation to use them to accomplish his redemptive purposes in this world. But this promise is not just for preachers and Old Testament professors. God calls kindergarten teachers, high school teachers, office administrators, businesspeople, social workers, nurses, and so forth.

God called Joshua to do what Moses could not do. How could he possibly do that? He knew he could not. But he trusted God's promise to be with him as he had been with Moses. And he obeyed God. You know the rest of the story.

Are you willing to hear God's gracious invitation to do what you know you cannot do in your own strength? Are you willing to trust that the same God who used Moses—the illegal son of despised immigrants—will be with you as you trust and obey him? You may not perform the same signs and wonders God did through Moses. Joshua didn't.

You are not called to be Moses or Joshua or Wendell Bowes. But God invites each of us to be his redemptive agents, using the gifts he has given us, to serve his purposes where we are or wherever he calls us to go.

Why should we think this encouragement applied to more people than just Joshua? Hear David's final instructions to his son Solomon, who was about to succeed him on the throne of Israel: "Be strong and of good courage, and act. Do not be afraid or dismayed; for the LORD God, my God, is with you. He will not fail you or forsake you" (1 Chron. 28:20, NRSV). Isaiah 41 applies this same promise to all God's faithful people: "Do not fear, for I am with you, do not be afraid, for I am your God; I will strengthen you, I will help you, I will uphold you with my victorious right hand. . . . For I, the LORD your God, hold your right hand; it is I who say to you, 'Do not fear, I will help you'" (vv. 10, 13, NRSV).

So, go, do the impossible, if that is what God has called you to do. God will be with you. Count on it. And if God is with you, you will lack nothing you need (Deut. 2:7). "Know therefore that the LORD your God is God, the faithful God who maintains covenant loyalty with those who love him and keep his commandments, to a thousand generations" (7:9, NRSV). "Have no dread of [those who oppose you], for the LORD your God, who is present with you, is a great and awesome God" (v. 21, NRSV). "The LORD your God who goes with you, to fight for you against your enemies, [will] give you victory" (20:4, NRSV).

God "will not fail you or forsake you." So "be strong and courageous" (Josh. 1:5-6, NRSV). I believe this would be Wendell's message to you members of his bereaved family, who are still trying to make sense of his untimely death: God will not fail or forsake you. Be strong and courageous because God is with you, as he was with Moses and Joshua and Wendell.

REFERENCES

Anderson, Bernhard W. 1986. *Understanding the Old Testament*. 4th ed. Englewood Cliffs, NJ: Prentice-Hall.

Atkins, Gaius Glenn. 1956. "The Book of Ecclesiastes: Exposition." Pages 1-88 in vol. 5 of *The Interpreter's Bible*, edited by George Arthur Buttrick. New York: Abingdon.

Balentine, Samuel E. 2018. *Wisdom Literature*. Core Biblical Studies. Nashville: Abingdon.

Bartholomew, Craig G., and Ryan P. O'Dowd. 2011. *Old Testament Wisdom Literature: A Theological Introduction*. Downers Grove, IL: InterVarsity.

Bennett, Stephen J. 2010. *Ecclesiastes/Lamentations: A Commentary in the Wesleyan Tradition*. New Beacon Bible Commentary. Kansas City: Beacon Hill Press of Kansas City.

Bowes, A. Wendell. 2018. *Job: A Commentary in the Wesleyan Tradition*. New Beacon Bible Commentary. Kansas City: Beacon Hill Press of Kansas City.

———. 2021. *Consider My Servant Job: An Interpretive Guide for Preachers and Teachers*. Kansas City: Foundry.

———. 2024. *The Wisdom Literature*. Reading and Interpreting the Bible Series. Kansas City: Foundry.

———. 2025. *Half Full: An Interpretive Guide to Proverbs*. Kansas City: Foundry.

Brown, William P. 2011. *Ecclesiastes*. Interpretation: A Bible Commentary for Teaching and Preaching. Louisville, KY: Westminster John Knox.

Brueggemann, Walter. 2019. *Preaching from the Old Testament*. Minneapolis: Fortress.

Childs, Brevard S. 1979. *Introduction to the Old Testament as Scripture*. Philadelphia: Fortress.

Clifford, Richard J. 1998. *The Wisdom Literature*. Interpreting Biblical Texts. Nashville: Abingdon.

Collins, John J. 1980. *Proverbs, Ecclesiastes*. Knox Preaching Guides. Atlanta: John Knox.

Crenshaw, James L. 1987. *Ecclesiastes*. The Old Testament Library. Philadelphia: Westminster.

———. 2010. *Old Testament Wisdom: An Introduction*. 3rd ed. Louisville, KY: Westminster John Knox.

———. 2017a. *Sipping from the Cup of Wisdom*. Vol. 1, *Exploring Diverse Paths of Research*. Macon, GA: Smyth and Helwys.

————. 2017b. *Sipping from the Cup of Wisdom*. Vol. 2, *Faith Lingering on the Edges*. Macon, GA: Smyth and Helwys.

Davidson, Robert. 1986. *Ecclesiastes and the Song of Solomon*. The Daily Study Bible Series. Louisville, KY: Westminster John Knox.

Davis, Ellen F. 2000. *Proverbs, Ecclesiastes, and the Song of Songs*. Westminster Bible Companion. Louisville, KY: Westminster John Knox.

Duncan, Julie Ann. 2017. *Ecclesiastes*. Abingdon Old Testament Commentaries. Nashville: Abingdon.

Eaton, Michael A. 1983. *Ecclesiastes: An Introduction and Commentary*. The Tyndale Old Testament Commentaries. Leicester, UK: Inter-Varsity.

Enns, Peter. 2008. "Ecclesiastes 1: Book of." Pages 121-32 in *Dictionary of the Old Testament: Wisdom, Poetry and Writings*, edited by Tremper Longman III and Peter Enns. Downers Grove, IL: InterVarsity.

Farmer, Kathleen A. 1991. *Who Knows What Is Good? A Commentary on the Books of Proverbs and Ecclesiastes*. International Theological Commentary. Grand Rapids: Eerdmans.

Fox, Michael V. 1999. *A Time to Tear Down and a Time to Build Up: A Rereading of Ecclesiastes*. Eugene, OR: Wipf and Stock.

————. 2004. *Ecclesiastes: The Traditional Hebrew Text with the New JPS Translation/Commentary by Michael V. Fox*. The JPS Bible Commentary. Philadelphia: The Jewish Publication Society.

Freedman, David Noel, ed. 1992. *The Anchor Bible Dictionary*. 6 vols. New York: Doubleday.

Gaither, William, and Gloria Gaither. 1975. "We Have This Moment, Today." Musicnotes.com. https://www.musicnotes.com/sheetmusic/mtd.asp?ppn=MN0152485.

Goldingay, John. 2014. *Proverbs, Ecclesiastes, and Song of Songs for Everyone*. Old Testament for Everyone. Louisville, KY: Westminster John Knox.

Gordis, Robert. 1968. *Koheleth—the Man and His World: A Study of Ecclesiastes*. 3rd ed. New York: Schocken.

Gowan, Donald E. 1980. *Reclaiming the Old Testament for the Christian Pulpit*. Edinburgh: T. and T. Clark.

Greathouse, William M., with George Lyons. 2008. *Romans 1–8: A Commentary in the Wesleyan Tradition*. New Beacon Bible Commentary. Kansas City: Beacon Hill Press of Kansas City.

Heim, Knut Martin. 2019. *Ecclesiastes: An Introduction and Commentary*. Tyndale Old Testament Commentaries 18. Downers Grove, IL: InterVarsity.

Horne, Milton P. 2003. *Proverbs, Ecclesiastes*. Smyth and Helwys Bible Commentary. Macon, GA: Smyth and Helwys.

Hunter, Alastair. 2006. *Wisdom Literature*. SCM Core Text. London: SCM.

Kidner, Derek. 1976. *The Message of Ecclesiastes: A Time to Mourn and a Time to Dance*. The Bible Speaks Today. Leicester, UK: Inter-Varsity.

———. 1985. *The Wisdom of Proverbs, Job and Ecclesiastes*: *An Introduction to Wisdom Literature*. Downers Grove, IL: InterVarsity.

Krüger, Thomas. 2004. *Qoheleth: A Commentary*. Hermeneia. Translated by O. C. Dean Jr. Minneapolis: Fortress.

Lambert, W. G. 1960. *Babylonian Wisdom Literature*. Oxford, UK: Oxford University Press. Reprint, Winona Lake, IN: Eisenbrauns, 1996.

Lichtheim, Miriam. 1973–2006. *Ancient Egyptian Literature: A Book of Readings*. 3 vols. Berkeley, CA: University of California Press.

Lodahl, Michael. 1994. *The Story of God: Wesleyan Theology and Biblical Narrative*. Kansas City: Beacon Hill Press of Kansas City.

Longman, Tremper, III. 1998. *The Book of Ecclesiastes*. The New International Commentary on the Old Testament. Grand Rapids: Eerdmans.

———. 2010. "Preaching Wisdom." Pages 102-21 in *Reclaiming the Old Testament for Christian Preaching*, edited by Grenville J. R. Kent, Paul J. Kissling, and Laurence A. Turner. Downers Grove, IL: InterVarsity.

McLaughlin, John L. 2018. *An Introduction to Israel's Wisdom Traditions*. Grand Rapids: Eerdmans.

Miller, Patrick D. 2009. *The Ten Commandments*. Interpretation: Resources for the Use of Scripture in the Church. Louisville, KY: Westminster John Knox.

Murphy, Roland E. 1992. *Ecclesiastes*. Word Biblical Commentary 23A. Nashville: Thomas Nelson.

Ogden, Graham S., and Lynell Zogbo. 1998. *A Handbook on Ecclesiastes*. UBS Handbook Series. New York: United Bible Societies.

Pauw, Amy Plantinga. 2015. *Proverbs and Ecclesiastes*. Belief: A Theological Commentary on the Bible. Louisville, KY: Westminster John Knox.

Perdue, Leo G. 2007. *Wisdom Literature: A Theological History*. Louisville, KY: Westminster John Knox.

———. 2008. *The Sword and the Stylus: An Introduction to Wisdom in the Age of Empires*. Grand Rapids: Eerdmans.

Pritchard, James B., ed. 1969. *Ancient Near Eastern Texts Relating to the Old Testament*. 3rd ed. with supplement. Princeton, NJ: Princeton University Press.

Rad, Gerhard von. 1972. *Wisdom in Israel*. Translated by James D. Martin. Nashville: Abingdon.

Rankin, O. S. 1956. "The Book of Ecclesiastes: Introduction and Exegesis." Pages 1-88 in vol. 5 of *The Interpreter's Bible*, edited by George Arthur Buttrick. New York: Abingdon.

Scott, R. B. Y. 1965. *Proverbs, Ecclesiastes: Introduction, Translation, and Notes*. The Anchor Bible 18. Garden City, NY: Doubleday.

———. 1971. *The Way of Wisdom in the Old Testament*. New York: Macmillan.

Seow, Choon-Leong. 1997. *Ecclesiastes: A New Translation with Introduction and Commentary*. The Anchor Bible 18C. New York: Doubleday.

Tobin, Thomas H. 1992. "Logos." Pages 348-56 in vol. 4 of *The Anchor Bible Dictionary*, edited by David Noel Freedman. New York: Doubleday.

Towner, W. Sibley. 1997. "The Book of Ecclesiastes: Introduction, Commentary, and Reflections." Pages 265-360 in vol. 5 of *The New Interpreter's Bible*, edited by Leander E. Keck. Nashville: Abingdon.

Treier, Daniel J. 2011. *Proverbs and Ecclesiastes*. Brazos Theological Commentary on the Bible. Grand Rapids: Brazos.

Vincent, Cory. 2019. "Three Reasons You Are Wrong about 'The Good Old Days.'" Ascent Publication. March 7, 2019. https://medium.com/the-ascent/3-reasons-you-are-wrong-about-the-good-old-days-e868973f37a9.

Viorst, Judith. 1972. *Alexander and the Terrible, Horrible, No Good, Very Bad Day*. New York: Atheneum.

Weeks, Stuart. 2010. *An Introduction to the Study of Wisdom Literature*. T. and T. Clark Approaches to Biblical Studies. London: T. and T. Clark.

Welch, Reuben. 1973. *We Really Do Need Each Other*. Nashville: Impact Books.

Wesley, John. 1760. "The Use of Money." Pages 348-57 in *John Wesley's Sermons: An Anthology*, edited by Albert C. Outler and Richard P. Heitzenrater. Nashville: Abingdon, 1991.

———. 1765. *Explanatory Notes upon the Old Testament*. Vol. 3. Bristol: William Pine.

Westermann, Claus. 1995. *Roots of Wisdom: The Oldest Proverbs of Israel and Other Peoples*. Translated by J. Daryl Charles. Louisville, KY: Westminster John Knox.

Witherington, Ben, III. 1994. *Jesus the Sage: The Pilgrimage of Wisdom*. Minneapolis: Fortress.